SIMPLE GOOD FOOD

SIMPLE GOOD FOOD

FUSION FOOD AT HOME WITH A FOUR-STAR CHEF

JEAN-GEORGES VONGERICHTEN

and MARK BITTMAN

photographs by

QUENTIN BACON

KYLE CATHIE LIMITED

First published in Great Britain in 1999 by
Kyle Cathie Limited
20 Vauxhall Bridge Road, London SW1V 2SA

First published 1998 by Broadway Books, New York

ISBN 1 85626 343 6

Jean-Georges Vongerichten and Mark Bittman are hereby identified
as the authors of this work in accordance with Section 77 of the
Copyright, Designs and Patents Act, 1988

A Cataloguing in Publication record for this title is available from the British Library

Designed by VERTIGO DESIGN, NYC
Photography by QUENTIN BACON
Food Styling by SUZIE SMITH
Printed and bound by TIEN WAH PRESS, SINGAPORE

ACKNOWLEDGMENTS

We had a tremendous amount of help in putting together this book, and so many people made the process a pleasant and even efficient one. We'd like to thank all of them.

Among those who work in what's called 'the front of the house,' Christian Carrere, Lois Freedman, Phillipe Gouze, Sue Kim, Alain Michel and Oliver Wharton smoothed the way for us. Guy Rabarijaona was always there when we needed him. Agnes Deshayes, Eric Precigoux and Patrick Van Den Bergh, all new additions, were incredibly helpful toward the end of the process.

Behind the scenes were the cooks and chefs who gave us a hand when we needed one, despite daily routines that are sometimes almost overwhelmingly demanding: Chris Beischer, Wylie Dufresne, Josh Eden, Ron Gallo, Elizabeth de Givenchy, Paulette Hawkins, Jonathan Pratt and Keith Williams. We were always grateful for the special help of the talented butcher Creseciano Torres. And although we were separated from them by oceans, we also were assisted by Dan Del Vecchio, Sean Guilmore, Poncho Gatchilian and Bruno Schoeffer. Special thanks go to Richard Farnabe, Pierre Shutz, Didier Virot and Keith Williams for their very concrete help all through this process.

We needed and received plenty of help from pastry chefs Eric Hubert and Serge Decrauzat, and their assistants Jon Anderson and Jehangir Mehta were great to work with.

On the business side of things, our jobs were made easier by Selene Ahn, Pearl Hsu, Sherry Hodes, Marie Marco, Ana Marie Mormando, Christian Nicolas, Raymond Pagares, Robert Riley, Kerri Simon, Rudy Tauscher and Joan Ward. Geralyn Delaney helped us in countless ways, and our agent, Angela Miller, got the ball rolling for us and cracked the whip when necessary.

The people who worked directly on producing this book all did a great job, but we'd especially like to thank Caitlin Connelly, Roberto de Vicq de Cumptich, Alexis Levenson, Alison Lew, John Sterling and Bill Shinker. Our editor, Harriet Bell, made perfect suggestions at every stage of the game and never missed a beat. Quentin Bacon and Suzie Smith produced the splendid photography you see here.

There are also some people who were especially helpful to each of us in our work in producing this book, or at least in our individual lives during its production, and we'd like to mention them too.

Jean-Georges Vongerichten and Mark Bittman

My special thanks go to Bob Giraldi and Phil Suarez, who have been with me and behind me for the last decade. Then there's my chiropractor, Dr. Drew DeMann, who kept me going when nothing else could. And, of course, Minh Nguyen and Philippe Vongerichten. Finally, there's Mark Bittman, without whom this book would not have existed.

Jean-Georges Vongerichten

I'd like to acknowledge my immediate family – Karen Baar, Emma Baar-Bittman, and Kate Baar-Bittman – who were enormously supportive during the time I spent away from home while working with Jean-Georges, and who were 'forced' to eat all the food resulting from our cooking sessions. Extra thanks to Harriet Bell and Angela Miller. And finally, to Jean-Georges, who is not only a brilliant chef but a fine person.

Mark Bittman

CONTENTS

INTRODUCTION

In the years before we agreed to produce this cookbook, I had worked occasionally with Jean-Georges Vongerichten and eaten at his restaurants more times than I could count, so I was prepared for both the brilliance of his food and his pleasant demeanour. Yet during our year of cooking together and assembling this book, Jean-Georges never failed to surprise me with his fierce determination to always get things right, his quick and sparkling wit, his supreme confidence at the stove and his warmth towards and respect for his employees and fellow workers. For those readers who have not had close encounters with chefs, let me assure you that this is an unusual, if not unique, combination.

That same phrase – 'unusual, if not unique' – best serves to describe Jean-Georges's food. It's generally agreed among food writers, restaurant critics and loyal customers that his cooking is highly creative without being weird, and intensely flavourful despite its simplicity. It is sometimes described as 'intellectual' food, which implies that a certain understanding of food and cooking is necessary in order to appreciate what Jean-Georges does. This is utter nonsense: Jean-Georges's combinations are novel, brilliant, even startling, but they are instantly appealing to anyone who likes to eat and is willing to sample new flavours.

Best yet, Jean-Georges's recipes are readily accessible to the home cook; in fact, most of them are easy. When we agreed to work together, I challenged him to preserve the flavours of his food while making the recipes simple enough for home cooks to prepare. His response at the time was immediate: 'We don't have to do anything; the food is easy already,'

and he patiently walked me through the restaurants' menus, discussing each dish and detailing how they were assembled. And, with very few exceptions, the recipes sounded as if they could be taken straight from the kitchens of his three restaurants, Vong, Jean-Georges, and JoJo (where the kitchen is, in fact, no bigger than the average home kitchen) and executed at home.

On that particular day, he demonstrated for me two sauces that had become recent passions. The first was a combination of mustard powder, sugar and water, which he was drizzling on a cabbage salad with great effect (you'll find the recipe on page 44). The second was a strange-sounding mixture of capers and raisins, which has since become part of a signature scallop-and-cauliflower dish at Jean-Georges (page 60). I found both encouraging but needed to know more. In the past, I've found many chefs who claim they produce accessible recipes, but when it comes right down to it, they say things like, 'You can't possibly make this sauce without foie gras,' or 'This dish isn't worth eating unless you use crème fraîche.' So I scheduled some time to cook with Jean-Georges and made a list of recipes I wanted to try. Among them were some of my favourites: Beetroot and Ginger Salad, Rice Paper Rolls of Shrimps and Herbs, Sautéed Chicken with Green Olives and Coriander (which has been on the JoJo menu from its opening), and the mysterious Steak with Red Wine Reduction and Carrot Purée. We worked alone, without help – which means we did all of our own peeling, chopping and other prepping.

When we got through the first two recipes, I realized that Jean-Georges wasn't kidding: many of his recipes contain only a few ingredients, and more than a few take less than a half hour to prepare. The Steak with Red Wine Reduction and Carrot Purée, which has intrigued me for years, is a perfect example. When I asked Jean-Georges how to make it, he said, 'You reduce a bottle of wine to a cup and you stir in carrot puree.' 'That's it?' 'That's it,' he insisted, with an impish grin. We made the two-ingredient sauce, added a little salt to it and spooned it over a grilled steak; it was sensational (as it was the next day, left over, on grilled pork). I soon came to learn that 'that's it' was a signature phrase for Jean-Georges; when other chefs would just be gearing up, his dishes were already done. They not only sound simple – note the recipe titles – they *are* simple.

At the end of the day, we were both surprised at how few compromises were necessary to adapt these recipes to the home kitchen. (In fact, we discovered many changes we could make to actually improve the recipes, given the flexibility of the home cook compared to that of the restaurant cook.)

Perhaps this was to be expected, because although he has reached the top level of his profession, Jean-Georges is a home cook at heart. His first teacher was his mother, he has a solid grounding in peasant food, he loves simple, intense flavours (and a whole range of textures), and he is constantly striving to make things easier. In the '80s, when he had a reputation to earn, he spent days preparing elaborate oils and combinations of oils. Now he achieves the same flavours by combining herbs and spices in the saucepan, frying pan or blender. Or he makes uncommon sauces, sometimes with common ingredients – like capers and raisins. 'It seems to get simpler and easier,' he says.

Jean-Georges is always on to something new, and what he tries usually works; he amasses concepts the way other chefs do recipes and he never stops experimenting with new flavours. For him even failure breeds success: 'I cannot know the best use for a flavour until I try it in every way that might make sense,' he says.

But he doesn't like to fuss. Like any busy cook, he looks for shortcuts, and he finds them. He is full of delightful surprises and, regardless of whether you are familiar with his cooking, you will find those surprises throughout this book.

There are, of course, many other chefs who combine classic European training with the flavours of the rest of the world, but Jean-Georges was among the first and he came by it honestly. Born in rural Alsace – itself a region of fusion food, since it straddles France and Germany – Jean-Georges grew up eating traditional food cooked by his grandmother and mother. As a teenager, he aspired to cook for the work-crew of his grandfather's coal business, but his parents had higher ambitions and sent him to cooking school.

At sixteen, he was cooking at the three-star (these are Michelin stars – they only go up to three) L'Auberge de L'Ill, generally considered Alsace's best restaurant. He remained there for four years, then went on to work with Paul Bocuse, Eckart Witzigmann (in Munich) and, finally, with Louis Outhier of L'Oasis on the French Riviera. It was Outhier's genius that set Jean-Georges on his true path by sending him to the United States and Asia as leader of his 'flying squadron' of chefs. Ultimately, Jean-Georges cooked for four years in Asia, spending time in Bangkok, Singapore and Hong Kong. As he now says, 'The flavours of lemongrass, ginger, coriander and coconut milk changed my life'. At the time, none of those flavours were being used by French-trained chefs in France, and to this day many traditional French chefs consider blending Asian or other non-European flavours with more traditional ones little short of heresy.

In 1984, Outhier sent Jean-Georges to Boston to become chef of the new Marquis restaurant. There, Jean-Georges unveiled a personal cuisine that synthesised East and West in unmatched fashion, and the Marquis was almost instantly named Boston's best French restaurant. This success was duplicated in 1986, when he became chef at Restaurant Lafayette in Midtown Manhattan. Lafayette was given three stars by *The New York Times* in its first review and the paper's highest rating – four stars – came just two years later. Jean-Georges was using Asian flavours then, but the real raves were for his elaborate flavoured oils, juice-based reductions, and other high-flavour, low-fat seasonings.

Since then, no discussion of New York's top restaurants has been complete without mention of Jean-Georges. By the time he left Lafayette in 1990, classic French cuisine was barely in his repertoire and his cooking was admired and emulated everywhere.

His rise, which was swift up until then, became meteoric. In 1991, Jean-Georges opened JoJo, a relatively simple restaurant – some call it a bistro – in which he serves French food strongly influenced by Asian flavours. Vong, which opened a year later, is often called a Thai restaurant; on closer

examination, its cooking is southeast Asian at its core, strongly influenced by French flavours. Taken together, the restaurants form the core of Jean-Georges's cuisine.

Both restaurants opened to national acclaim and remain enormously popular. (There are now Vongs in London and Hong Kong.) In the autumn of 1996, it was announced (and was front-page news) that Jean-Georges won the informal competition to run the restaurant in the completely remodelled One Central Park West, the dominant structure in Columbus Circle, dividing Midtown and the Upper West Side. The restaurant opened in March and, about three months later, was given four stars by the *Times*.

Jean-Georges's current food can be called 'global basic,' a style that did not – indeed could not – exist before, because ingredients and techniques have only recently become universal. Jean-Georges's palette draws from everywhere and his palate appreciates everything; I've yet to find a flavour he doesn't enjoy.

By now you've gathered, if you didn't know already, that not all of Jean-Georges's ingredients are found in the typical Western kitchen. Surprisingly, however, most of them – including lemongrass,

 ginger, coriander, coconut milk, 'exotic' mushrooms, and almost every dried spice imaginable – can be found in the typical supermarket. You can find a glossary of ingredients used in this book with which you might not be familiar beginning on page 188.

But if your shopping trips take a little longer than they once did, your cooking times may be shorter. Although this is not a brilliant-food-in-twenty-minutes cookbook, there are plenty of recipes here that can be cooked on after a day's work. Those that take longer are worth the effort.

Similarly, this is not a low-fat cookbook, but it's worth noting that many of Jean-Georges's preparations are extremely low in fat. However, neither of us is interested in eliminating butter or other fats when such a change would

compromise flavour. Wherever appropriate, we point out those places where oils high in poly- and/or mono-unsaturated fats can be used in place of butter.

In short, this is one chef's book that should serve to delight rather than frustrate you. I intend to continue to cook from it for years to come.

Mark Bittman

SIMPLE GOOD FOOD

FIRST COURSES

Jean-Georges turns a rather common combination – tomatoes and basil – into something unique and beautitiful. And the basil oil is an elegant finishing touch.

You can go in many directions after this light first course, but perhaps meat is best. If you're grilling, try Steak with Red Wine Reduction and Carrot Purée (page 112); or, if the weather is cool, Lamb Chops with Root Vegetables and Horseradish (page 116).

SERVES 4

TOMATO TOWERS
WITH BASIL

4 large tomatoes
Salt and freshly ground black pepper
Sherry vinegar
About 2 large handfuls basil leaves
125ml/4fl oz extra virgin olive oil

1 Bring a pot of water to the boil. Core the tomatoes, then make a small 'X' on their bottom (flower) end. Drop them into the boiling water and remove when their skins begin to loosen, about 30 seconds later. Drain, then immediately submerge the tomatoes into a large bowl of iced water. When cool, peel them, then cut horizontally into 4 or 5 thick slices. Discard the bottom slice of each tomato, but keep the other slices in order; they're going to be restacked. Sprinkle each of the slices with salt, pepper and a few drops of sherry vinegar.

2 Drop half the basil leaves into boiling water for 10 seconds, then remove and rinse in cold water immediately. Place them, still wet, in a blender; with the motor running, and drizzle in the olive oil.

3 On individual plates, reassemble the tomatoes with the flat side down, putting a basil leaf or two between each layer. Surround with a little basil oil, then sprinkle the whole thing with salt and garnish with a little more basil.

When Jean-Georges first served this minimalist first course at JoJo, customers balked; they wanted mushrooms sautéed in butter. The conversion began when they caught a whiff of the pure mushroom aroma wafting through the dining room. Use any good mushrooms you have. Delicate chanterelles are best this way.

This should be followed by a big but somewhat rustic second course, such as Cranberry Beans with Seafood (page 70), Sautéed Chicken with Figs (page 87), or any meat dish.

SERVES 4

STEAMED CHANTERELLES WITH SHALLOTS AND SPROUTS

500g/1lb chanterelles or other mushrooms, or a mixture, trimmed and cleaned

1½ tablespoons minced shallots

Juice of 1 lemon

2½ tablespoons vegetable, grapeseed or other neutral-flavoured oil

Salt and freshly ground black pepper

4 large handfuls mixed salad greens

50g/2oz sprouts, such as alfalfa, cress or radish

Minced chives

1 Place the chanterelles in the top level of a steamer and cook over boiling water for 5 minutes. Remove the mushrooms, then toss them in a bowl with the shallots. Add the lemon juice and oil and toss again. Taste; keep the lemon juice to a minimum lest it overwhelm the mushrooms, but add some salt and a fair amount of pepper.

2 Toss together the greens and sprouts and divide the mixture among 4 plates. Top with the mushroom mixture. Garnish with chives and serve.

The first time I tasted these crisp stuffed titbits I begged Jean-Georges to cook them with me the next day.

They're not exactly ravioli, but sautéed potato pockets filled with mushroom stuffing.

Serve them as finger food or plated with a green salad. Like 'real'

ravioli, you may fill them with anything you like. One caveat: you

must use a mandoline to slice the potatoes thinly enough.

POTATO 'RAVIOLI'

3 large baking potatoes (about 750g/1½lb), each as long and wide as you can find

Extra virgin olive oil

500g/1lb mushrooms (any combination, such as half shiitake, half button)

1½ tablespoons butter

6 garlic cloves, sliced

2 shallots, sliced

1 teaspoon thyme leaves

Salt and freshly ground black pepper

4–6 sprigs parsley leaves

1 egg yolk

1 Preheat the oven to 230°C/450°F/gas 8. Peel the potatoes, leaving one of the long ends of each unpeeled to give you a better grip. Slice the potatoes lengthwise on a mandoline; make the slices so thin you can see your hand through them. You should have at least 24 slices.

2 Line a baking tray with greaseproof paper or use a nonstick baking tray. Brush the paper or the sheet with olive oil and lay the potato slices on there as closely as you can without overlapping. You may need 2 baking trays.

3 Bake the potatoes until they are even more translucent and take on a pale yellow colour, for 10 to 20 minutes. They are done when they are tender and pliable but not at all brown (reduce the oven temperature if they begin to brown). Cool the tray(s) on a rack for a couple of minutes, then pat the potatoes dry with paper towels.

4 Meanwhile, trim, clean and destem the mushrooms (discard the stems of shiitakes; you can use the stems of other mushrooms). Place the butter in a large frying pan, turn the heat to high and add the mushrooms, garlic, shallots, thyme and a sprinkling of salt and pepper. Cook, stirring frequently, until the liquid has evaporated and the mushrooms are nicely browned, for about 15 minutes. Stir in the parsley.

5 Place the mushroom mixture in a food processor and pulse a few times, until coarsely chopped but not puréed. You will probably have to scrape down the mixture between pulses.

6 Beat the egg yolk in a bowl, then brush half the rim of a potato slice lightly with it. Place a scant teaspoon of stuffing in the centre of the slice, then fold over and seal. Repeat until all the slices are stuffed.

7 Place about 2 tablespoons olive oil in a large frying pan and turn the heat to high. Sauté the potato raviolis a few at a time until lightly browned on both sides; each will take only a minute or so per side. Keep warm until all are cooked, serve hot or warm.

Little short of magic: take leeks (preferably the more delicate leeks of spring), simmer until tender and use them to fill a mould. Press them down and the next day you have a terrine. 'Leeks have loads of natural gelatin,' says Jean-Georges. 'I just tried to create a dish that took advantage of that.' To make this, you will need a narrow rectangular mould, approximately the same length as the leeks – about 35cm/14in long by 7cm/3in wide by 7cm/3in high. It's worth buying one, although if you prefer not to, you can trim the leeks to fit whatever mould or loaf tin you have on hand.

The green-and-white terrine is especially fine with the truffle juice vinaigrette made for Asparagus Salad with Soy Vinaigrette and Hollandaise (page 40), but even a simple dressing, such as Lemon Vinaigrette (page 210), will do nicely. This is a light first course, so you can follow it with something filling, such as Baeckoffe of Pork (page 121) or Lobster with Pumpkin Seed Broth (page 66).

SERVES 12

 # LEEK TERRINE

2.5–3kg/5–6lb leeks

Salt and freshly ground black pepper

Any vinaigrette (pages 208–210) or extra virgin olive oil and lemon juice

1 Put a large pot of salted water on to boil. Leaving the root ends of the leeks intact (this will help keep them together), split them almost to the root; trim off any hard green parts and wash well. Use string to tie the leeks into 4 bundles; this, too, will keep them from falling apart. Plunge them into the boiling water and cook until very tender, for about 20 minutes (when done, a thin-bladed knife will pierce them easily).

2 Drain the leeks and let them cool for about 5 minutes. Meanwhile, line the terrine with enough clingfilm to fold over the top.

3 Trim the root ends from the leeks. If the leeks are 3cm/1in thick or more in diameter, split them in half; if not, leave them whole. Make one layer of leeks with the white ends facing toward you; then one with the white ends away from you. Repeat, alternating directions, until all the leeks are used. You can go about 3cm/1in over the top of the terrine but no more.

4 Bring the clingfilm up over the top of the leeks, but leave an opening to allow liquid to run out. Place a flat piece of wood or heavy cardboard that will fit snugly inside the mould on top of the leeks. Place two or three custard cups or ramekins on a baking sheet with a lip, and invert the mould so that the wood or cardboard rests directly on the cups; you want to elevate the mold a bit over the baking sheet so the liquid drains away from the terrine.

5 Invert the terrine so that it is right-side up. Refrigerate for 24 hours. You will note that the leeks are packed almost as solid as a brick.

6 Invert the mould again, this time onto a cutting board; then unmould, but leave wrapped in the plastic – this will be much easier than you might imagine. Trim the ragged edges, then use a serrated knife to slice right through the clingfilm. Discard the clingfilm, then place each slice on a plate. Sprinkle with salt and pepper, then dress with the vinaigrette. The unused portion of the terrine will keep, well-wrapped and refrigerated, for several days.

This joint collaboration between Jean-Georges and the talented Didier Virot, chef de cuisine at Restaurant Jean-Georges, was originally served at JoJo; it has been a smash hit there and at Jean-Georges. It's great with shiitakes but even better, of course, with fresh porcini, if you can find (and afford!) them.

Serve with some mixed greens dressed with Honey-Garlic Vinaigrette (page 209), and follow with any light, simple second course, such as Curried Mussels (page 59) or Dill-Stuffed Shrimps with Baked Lemon (page 63).

MAKES 4 TARTS

MUSHROOM TARTS WITH ONIONS AND WALNUTS

50g/2oz walnuts

1 tablespoon butter or extra virgin olive oil (5 tablespoons if you're using phyllo dough)

2 tablespoons vegetable, grapeseed or other neutral-flavoured oil

1 large onion, sliced

Salt

About 500g/1lb porcini or shiitake mushrooms, stems removed and discarded or reserved for stock (you can use the stems from fresh porcini, if you have them)

¼ teaspoon freshly ground black pepper

Four 15cm/6in rounds refrigerated Puff Pastry, page 184; or use commercial refrigerated puff pastry or 6 sheets phyllo dough

1 teaspoon minced garlic

1 Toast the walnuts in a dry frying pan over medium heat, shaking occasionally, until just beginning to brown, for about 5 minutes; set aside.

2 Meanwhile, fill with water a pot large enough to hold the mushrooms and put it on to boil. At the same time, place 1 tablespoon of the butter or olive oil and 1 tablespoon of the neutral-flavoured oil in a frying pan and turn the heat to high. Add the onion and a pinch of salt and cook, stirring occasionally, until the onion begins to brown, for about 5 minutes. Reduce the heat to medium-low and continue to cook, stirring occasionally, until the onion is tender but not mushy, 5 to 10 minutes more.

3 Place the mushrooms in the boiling water. Cook for 2 minutes, stirring occasionally. Drain, rinse, then drain again. (This process allows the mushrooms to release their excess water so they don't make the crust soggy when it bakes.)

4 Place the onion, walnuts and pepper in a food processor and pulse a few times. Make the mixture spreadable, but not quite a purée. You will have to scrape down the mixture between pulses. Preheat the oven to 200°C/400°F/gas 6.

5 If you're using puff pastry, place the circles on 1 or 2 baking trays lined with greaseproof paper (or use nonstick baking sheets) and poke them all over with a fork. If you're using phyllo, melt the remaining 5 tablespoons butter.

Brush a sheet of phyllo with butter, cover it with another sheet, brush that one and cover it with one more. Cut two 15 to 17cm/6 to 7in circles out of the dough, then repeat the process with three more sheets of phyllo to make a total of four circles. Brush the tops of the circles with melted butter or oil and place on 1 or 2 baking trays lined with greasproof paper (or use nonstick baking trays).

6   Spread each circle with a thin layer of the walnut-onion mixture, leaving a 2.5cm/1in border all around. Layer the mushrooms attractively on the spread.

7   Combine the minced garlic with the remaining 1 tablespoon vegetable oil. Brush the top of the tarts with about half of this mixture. Bake for 10 to 15 minutes, or until the edges of the tarts are brown. Remove from the oven and brush the tarts lightly with the garlic oil once again. Serve immediately.

You can make the dough and the filling for these tarts several hours – or even a day – in advance, which will leave a simple assembly and baking to do at the last minute.

At JoJo, these tarts are topped with a slice of bacon and a fried egg – a sensational presentation. If you follow that route, all you'll need to be satisfied is a lean salad, such as Fennel and Apple Salad with Juniper (page 48).

MAKES 4 TARTS

LEEK AND POTATO TARTS

200g/7oz flour, plus more for rolling out the dough

60ml/2fl oz plus 2 tablespoons extra virgin olive oil

Salt

1 large baking potato (a little more than 250g/½lb)

2 or 3 medium-to-large leeks (a little more than 250g/½lb), trimmed of hard green parts, split in half, and well washed

125ml/4fl oz milk

125ml/4fl oz double cream

Nutmeg

150g/5oz freshly grated Parmesan cheese

Coarse sea salt

1 Place the flour in a bowl. Make a well in the centre of the flour, and add the 4 tablespoons of oil, a pinch of salt and a scant 125ml/4fl oz water. Mix together with your hands, then spill onto a lightly floured board and knead until firm and elastic, for about 2 minutes; the dough should be just slightly sticky to the touch. Wrap in clingfilm and leave to rest for about 30 minutes at room temperature, or overnight in the refrigerator (bring back to room temperature before proceeding).

2 Cook the potato in boiling salted water until tender, at least 30 minutes. While it is cooking, cut the leeks into very fine dice, or chop them finely in a food processor (be careful not to purée them). Place the remaining 2 table-spoons olive oil in a 25cm/10in frying pan and turn the heat to medium. Add the leeks and a sprinkling of salt and cover; cook, stirring occasionally, until they are very tender, for about 12 minutes.

3 Peel the potato and mash it with a fork, leaving some small lumps. While it is still warm, place it in a small saucepan and pour the milk and cream over it. Turn the heat to medium-low and cook, stirring, for just a few minutes, until the liquid is absorbed and the mixture is thick. Stir in a pinch of nutmeg, the cooked leeks and the Parmesan. (This entire mixture, like the dough, can be made a day in advance and refrigerated; bring back to room temperature before proceeding.)

4 Preheat the oven to 200°C/400°F/gas 6. Divide the dough into 4. On a lightly floured surface, roll out one quarter as thinly as you can, adding

additional flour as needed. Use a plate to cut the dough into a circle of about 20cm/8in in diameter, then place $\frac{1}{4}$ of the filling in the centre. Brush the edges of the dough with water, then pinch the edges together over the filling, not enclosing it entirely. Place each finished tartlet on a greaseproof paper-lined or nonstick baking tray.

5 Bake the tartlets for 15 to 20 minutes, until nicely browned and bubbly. Sprinkle with coarse sea salt and serve hot or at room temperature.

Here, leaves of chard enclose a creamy filling to make an impressive first course. Yet you can assemble it a day (or even two) in advance, and steam it at the last minute. Do not substitute other greens for the chard; its distinctive flavour and texture define this dish.

Follow this with a simple second course, such as Roast Poussins with Herb-Bread Stuffing (page 96) or Sautéed Chicken with Prunes (page 88).

SERVES 4

SWISS CHARD TIMBALES

500g/1lb Swiss chard

Juice of 1 lemon

470ml/16fl oz cream

1 tablespoon minced garlic

50g/2oz freshly grated Parmesan cheese

1 egg yolk

½ teaspoon grated nutmeg

Salt and freshly ground black pepper

1 Cut along the stems of the chard to remove the leaves, keeping the leaves as intact as possible. Wash both stems and leaves. If the stems are thick, cut them the long way into 2 or 3 slices; if not, don't bother. Chop the stems into 5mm/¼in dice.

2 Bring 2 pots of salted water to the boil; add the juice of the lemon to one. Cook the stems in the acidulated water for about 10 minutes, until tender; drain. Cook the leaves in the other pot for 3 or 4 minutes until wilted and quite tender. Drain, then immediately submerge in a large bowl of iced water; when they're cool, drain them in a colander.

3 Combine the cream and the garlic in a small saucepan and cook over medium-high heat for about 15 minutes, or until reduced by more than half. Stir in the chard stems and reduce the heat to medium-low; cook for another 10 minutes or so, stirring occasionally. Cool the mixture for a few minutes, then stir in the Parmesan, egg yolk, nutmeg and salt and pepper to taste.

4 While the cream is reducing, line 4 large ramekins with clingfilm. Pat the chard leaves dry with kitchen roll, then line each of the plastic-lined cups with them, as few as 3 or 4 or as many as 6 or 7 per ramekin, depending on their size.

5 Fill the ramekins with the stem mixture and fold the leaves over; fold the plastic wrap over all. (You may prepare the recipe in advance up to this point; refrigerate for up to 2 days.)

6 Place in a steamer set over boiling water for 5 to 10 minutes (longer if the ramekins were refrigerated), until heated through; you can also microwave these, if you like. Carefully remove the chard packages from the clingfilm, place on small plates, and serve.

If you thought quiche was a delicate little dish, you're in for a surprise when you taste this gutsy combination.

As you might guess from glancing at the ingredients list, it's a filling appetizer – I find it perfect followed by Asparagus Salad with Soy Vinaigrette and Hollandaise (page 40). Or you might try Fresh Pea Soup (page 30).

SERVES 6 - 8

QUICHE OF CHICKEN LIVERS AND MUSHROOMS

90g/3oz flour, plus more for kneading and rolling

Salt

2½ tablespoons butter, softened, plus more for the pan

1 egg yolk

3 tablespoons sunflower, grapeseed or other neutral-flavoured oil

500g/1lb chicken livers, trimmed and cut into 1.2cm/½in dice

1 shallot, peeled and minced

375g/¾lb chanterelles, shiitakes or other mushrooms, trimmed (discard the stems of shiitakes or reserve them for stock) and coarsely chopped

250ml/9fl oz whipping cream

2 eggs

¼ teaspoon freshly grated nutmeg

1 tablespoon chopped chives

90g/3oz freshly grated Parmesan cheese

Freshly ground black pepper

1 Mix the flour with a pinch of salt in a medium bowl. Add 3 tablespoons of butter and squeeze through your fingers quickly and repeatedly until well blended. Stir in the egg yolk and 1 tablespoon of cold water and continue to mix; add a little more water if necessary to shape the mixture into a ball. Knead briefly on a lightly floured surface, just until smooth – you do not want to toughen the dough.

2 Roll out the dough on a lightly floured surface until it is 3mm/⅛in thick. Butter a 25cm/10in quiche or tart tin, preferably one with a removable base. Transfer the dough to the tin and trim the edges. Refrigerate for about 30 minutes.

3 Preheat the oven to 200°C/400°F/gas 6. Place 1 tablespoon of the oil in a 25cm/10in frying pan and turn the heat to medium-high. A minute later, add the livers and cook, stirring occasionally, until they lose their surface colour, about 2 minutes. Scoop them out of the pan and set aside. Wipe out the pan.

4 Place the remaining 2 tablespoons of oil in the pan, increase the heat to high, and add the shallot. A minute later, add the mushrooms. Cook, stirring occasionally, for about 10 minutes, until the mushroom liquid evaporates and the mushrooms begin to brown.

5 Mix together the cream, eggs, nutmeg, chives and Parmesan; add salt and pepper to taste. Scatter the mushrooms and the livers in the tart shell, then fill almost to the brim with the egg mixture. Bake for 20 to 30 minutes, or until the mixture is firm but still a little jiggly in the middle. Leave to rest for 10 minutes before cutting and serving.

Spring rolls made of rice paper are impressive, easily assembled and versatile. Once you learn to make these rolls, you'll be stuffing them with whatever is on hand. Be sure to practise on your family or friends, though, before making rice paper rolls for your boss; they won't look great until you've had a little practice. Once you've mastered the basic technique, the possibilities are endless: substitute raw tuna or cooked salmon for the shrimps, add avocado and/or bean sprouts to the mix, eliminate the seafood entirely and make a vegetarian roll, or vary the quantities of the ingredients.

You can make these up to a day ahead and store them in clingfilm in the refrigerator; let them come to room temperature before serving. They're fine finger food, but if you're making them for a sit-down dinner, follow them with something substantial, such as Poached Fish with Fennel (page 76) or Duck à la JoJo (page 100).

SERVES 4

RICE PAPER ROLLS OF SHRIMP AND HERBS

About 200g/7oz rice vermicelli

8 to 12 medium-to-large shrimps

4 sheets rice paper, 20–25cm/8–10in in diameter

125g/4oz grated, shredded, or julienned carrot

2 spring onions, white part with a little of the green, trimmed and cut into slivers the long way

1 small (pickling) cucumber, peeled and cut into thin strips or shredded

20 or more mint leaves

About 8 coriander sprigs

5-Minute Dipping Sauce (page 201)

1 Soak the rice noodles in fairly hot water (about 50°C/120°F, almost too hot to touch) for 10 to 20 minutes, or until soft. Drain thoroughly.

2 Meanwhile, prepare the other ingredients. Steam or simmer the shrimps over or in boiling water for 3 minutes or until pink. Run them under cold water for a few seconds to stop the cooking, then peel and cut into 2 slices each.

3 Have all the ingredients in one place; you'll also need a bowl of hot water (45°–50°C/110°–120°F) and clean kitchen roll. Put a sheet of rice paper into the water for about 20 seconds, just until soft (don't let it become too soft; it will continue to soften as you work). Lay it on the kitchen roll.

4 In the middle of the rice paper, lay 2 or 3 shrimps and about a quarter each of the noodles, carrot, spring onions and cucumber. Do not overfill. Top with mint and coriander; don't skimp on the herbs.

5 Working quickly, roll up the rice paper, keeping it fairly tight. Now roll the rice paper roll in a sheet of clingfilm, again making it tight. Fold over the last bit of clingfilm in the opposite direction, forming a tab that will make it easy to unwrap. Twist the ends and serve or store, refrigerated, for up to a day.

6 To serve, trim the ends of each roll with a sharp knife, then cut into 2.5cm/1in sections, right through the plastic wrap. Unwrap each section and place, cut side up, on a plate. Serve with the dipping sauce.

Crisp, hot and simple, these were one of the original Vong appetisers and have never left the menu. They're best with Tamarind Dipping Sauce (page 200), but if you're pressed for time, use the 5-Minute Dipping Sauce (page 201) or just plain soy sauce.

To continue the meal in the spirit of this dish, follow it with Beef with Ginger (page 110), Pork in Caramel Sauce (page 120), or Chicken with Lemongrass (page 90).

MAKES ABOUT 15, ENOUGH FOR 5 TO 15 SERVINGS

CRAB SPRING ROLLS

500g/1lb crabmeat, picked over and shredded

1 tablespoon mayonnaise

Fifteen 20cm/8in square spring roll or egg roll wrappers

2 egg yolks, lightly beaten

Vegetable, grapeseed or other neutral-flavoured oil, for deep frying

15 small, tender Iceberg lettuce leaves

Mint and coriander leaves

1 Mix the crabmeat with the mayonnaise. Place one of the spring roll wrappers on a work surface, with a point facing you. Spoon a heaping tablespoon of the mixture into the centre of the wrapper, making a 10cm/4in log from left to right. Fold over the left and right corners, so that they meet in the middle and one overlaps the other. Brush a bit of the egg yolk over the top half of the wrapper. Fold the bottom half up, then roll tightly; the yolk will seal the spring roll. (You may prepare the spring rolls in advance up to this point; refrigerate, well-wrapped or in a covered container, for up to 2 hours.)

2 Heat the oil to 150°/365°F. Deep fry the spring rolls, 3 or 4 at a time, for 2 minutes or less, or until an appealing shade of brown. Drain on kitchen roll.

3 To serve, place each spring roll on a lettuce leaf and garnish with a few herb leaves.

Most shrimp satays are little more than skewered shrimps, but in Jean-Georges's hands, they become shrimps coated with fresh shrimp paste, then crisped up with toasted bread crumbs.

This *is* a starter – I like it followed by the easy Stir-Fried Chicken with Tamarind Glaze (page 95) – but two shrimp lovers could easily handle it as a main course.

SERVES 4

SHRIMP SATAY

24 medium-to-large shrimps, peeled and deveined

1 teaspoon curry paste, All-Purpose Curry Powder (page 214), or commercial curry powder

2 teaspoons nam pla or nuoc mam (Asian fish sauce)

Salt and cayenne pepper

Coarse, freshly toasted bread crumbs

2½ tablespoons vegetable, grapeseed or other neutral-flavoured oil

Oyster Sauce (page 203), Sweet-and-Sour Sauce (page 215), or lime wedges

1 Combine half the shrimps, the curry paste or powder and the nam pla in a food processor. Process, stopping the machine and scraping down the sides as necessary, until the mixture is puréed. Refrigerate the mixture for at least 30 minutes, until it is stiff.

2 Place the remaining shrimps on 4 skewers, then season them with salt and cayenne to taste. Spread one side of the shrimp with the chilled purée, then dip into the bread crumbs. Repeat with the other side and place on wax paper; chill for at least 30 minutes to firm up. Preheat the oven to 250°C/475°F/gas 9.

3 Place the oil in a frying pan (preferably nonstick) large enough to hold the skewers and turn the heat to high. When the oil begins to smoke, add the skewers and cook for about 2 minutes, or until the shrimps are light brown. Turn over the shrimps, then place the frying pan in the oven for 2 or 3 minutes more. Return to the top of the stove and turn the skewers to brown briefly the edges of the shrimps.

4 Serve with Oyster Sauce, Sweet-and-Sour Sauce or lime wedges.

Orange Dust (page 211) is a potent, beguiling powder made from the peels of oranges; you can use it on any meat or seafood. Adding artichoke hearts to this dish – a staple on the menu at JoJo – may be gilding the lily, but the artichokes and their cooking liquid are a beautiful touch, so why not? If, however, you have neither artichokes nor time (and you have already made orange dust), try the shrimps, simply sautéed, garnished with basil, and placed on a bed of arugula.

Almost any second course will pale after this, so keep it simple: Roast Poussins with Herb-Bread Stuffing (page 96), for example, Roast Chicken Breasts with Pine or Rosemary (page 94), or informally, even Creamy Butternut Squash Soup (page 29).

SERVES 4

SAUTÉED SHRIMPS WITH ORANGE DUST

4 large globe artichokes

5 tablespoons extra virgin olive oil

1 medium onion, sliced

375ml/13fl oz dry white wine

Salt and freshly ground black pepper

Juice of 1/2 lemon

24 large shrimps (at least 500g/1lb), peeled

Cayenne pepper

3 tablespoons butter

Orange Dust (page 211)

3 to 4 large handfuls arugula

Minced fresh basil

1 Trim the artichokes: cut off their pointy tops to within 3–4cm/1–1½in of the base; remove all but about 1.2cm/½in of the stem. Cut all around the artichoke, removing all of the hard parts. Open up the centre and dig out the choke with a blunt-edged spoon. Trim any remaining hard parts; what's left is the artichoke bottom.

2 Place 4 tablespoons of oil in a large, deep frying pan and turn the heat to medium-high. Add the onion and cook, stirring, until it begins to soften, 2 or 3 minutes. Lay the artichoke bottoms on top of the onion, then pour in the wine. Bring to the boil, reduce the heat to low and cover. Simmer, turning over the artichokes after about 15 minutes, until the bottoms are tender but not mushy, 30 to 45 minutes total.

3 When the artichokes are done, remove them, reserving about 190ml/7fl oz of their cooking liquid. Cut them into bite-sized chunks and return them to the pan with the cooking liquid, remaining 1 tablespoon of olive oil, salt and pepper to taste, and the lemon juice. Turn the heat to very low to keep them warm.

4 Season each shrimp with salt and a tiny sprinkling of cayenne. Place a large nonstick frying pan over medium-high heat and, a minute later, add the butter. Dredge each of the shrimps in turn in the orange dust and place them in the frying pan. Cook for about 2 minutes, until lightly browned, then turn over carefully. Cook for another 2 minutes or so.

5 Divide the arugula among 4 plates. Top each with a portion of the artichokes and 6 shrimps; pour the artichoke liquid over all and garnish with basil. Sprinkle a little orange powder around the outside of each plate and serve immediately.

Lemongrass is one of Jean-Georges's favourite seasonings and everyone who works with him comes to love it. This dish, created by talented Vong sous-chef Keith Williams, employs it not only as a spice but as a skewer.

Serve the skewers, if you can, with Red Cabbage and Watercress Salad (page 45), and chew on the lemongrass stalks when you've done – a rustic delight.

TUNA SKEWERED WITH LEMONGRASS

5 stalks lemongrass

500–600g/1–1¼lb high-quality fresh tuna, cut into 12 large cubes

Freshly ground black pepper

1 tablespoon plus 2 teaspoons vegetable, grapeseed or other neutral-flavoured oil

1 small fresh chilli, minced, or dried red pepper flakes

Juice of 1 lime

2 teaspoons nam pla or nuoc mam (Asian fish sauce)

Pinch of sugar

Coarse sea salt

1 Trim the lemongrass of its outer sheath, then cut off the top 5cm/2in or so of the thick part. Bruise 4 of the stalks all over with the back of a knife. Remove another layer or two of the fifth stalk, then finely mince the tender inner core. Reserve all the trimmings.

2 Place 3 tuna cubes on each of the 4 intact stalks, leaving some space between each cube. Roll the tuna in the minced lemongrass, then sprinkle it with black pepper and drizzle it with 1 tablespoon of oil. Refrigerate the tuna and let it sit for at least an hour, preferably a day.

3 Chop all the lemongrass trimmings and measure them. Combine with an equal amount of water in a small saucepan. Cover and bring to the boil over high heat; cook, checking occasionally, for about 15 minutes, until reduced to about 2 tablespoons. Strain the liquid, then return it to the saucepan and reduce until it is only about 1 tablespoon.

4 Combine the lemongrass reduction with the chilli or dried red pepper flakes to taste, the lime juice, nam pla, sugar and remaining 2 teaspoons of oil. Set aside.

5 Start a charcoal fire in a grill or preheat a gas grill; the fire should be quite hot. Grill the tuna skewers for about a minute per side, until charred but quite rare. Spoon a little of the lemongrass sauce over each piece and top with sea salt. Serve.

Jean-Georges likes this signature Vong dish as an appetiser, but, with a greater amount of tuna and greens, it also makes for an informal main course.

Make sure the tuna is top-quality bluefin or yellowfin.

SEARED TUNA WITH SZECHWAN PEPPERCORNS

1 tablespoon Szechwan peppercorns

500–600g/1–1¼lb tuna steak, at least 3.5cm/1¼in thick

Salt

50g/2oz Dijon mustard

90ml/3fl oz soy sauce

Freshly ground black pepper

1 tablespoon minced shallot

2 tablespoons minced ginger

About 125ml/4fl oz vegetable, grapeseed or other neutral-flavoured oil

2 tablespoons lemon juice

4 to 6 handfuls mesclun or other mixed salad greens

1 Place the peppercorns on a cutting board. Crush them by pressing on them with the bottom of a heavy pot, then mince them with a knife. Cut the tuna steak into 4 rectangular steaks (the ends will be uneven, but that's okay), then roll the steaks lightly in the peppercorns. Sprinkle with salt.

2 Whisk together the mustard and soy sauce, then add some black pepper, along with the shallot, ginger, 4 tablespoons of oil and the lemon juice. Whisk again to emulsify.

3 Place a large frying pan over high heat and add enough oil to just film the bottom (the easiest way to do this is to add the entire remaining 4 table-spoons of oil, heat it a little, then pour most of it out). Add the tuna and cook for about 1 minute per side (a total of 4 minutes), just enough to char the outside; it should be quite rare.

4 Cut the tuna into 2-cm/½-thick slices and arrange them on 4 plates, each with a portion of greens and a small bowl of dipping sauce for dipping both tuna and greens. Serve at once.

When Pierre Schutz, who has been the innovative chef at Vong for several years, mentioned this dish to me, I was a little taken aback. Boiled potatoes topped with smoked salmon, surrounded by a creamy cucumber broth spiked with grapefruit is, after all, a strange-sounding combination. It turns out, however, to be one in which the flavours marry perfectly.

Consider this dish, which should be served at room temperature as soon as it is assembled, a large appetizer or a small main course. Follow it with the more assertive Scallops and Squid with Asian Spices, Paprika, and Butter (page 62).

SERVES 4

SALMON AND GRAPEFRUIT IN CUCUMBER MILK

4 round waxy potatoes, each about 4cm/1½in in diameter

1 tablespoon butter

1 English cucumber, unpeeled and chopped

Salt

250ml/9fl oz milk

20–25 mint leaves

1 pink or red grapefruit

2 tablespoons plain yogurt

¼ teaspoon Vong Chilli Paste (page 215) or cayenne pepper

375g/¾lb salmon fillet

1 tablespoon minced shallot

1 tablespoon vegetable, grapeseed or other neutral-flavoured oil

250g/8oz minced spinach or tender lettuce, such as Iceberg

Freshly ground black pepper

Lime wedges

Minced coriander for garnish

1 Simmer the potatoes in boiling salted water to cover, for 20 to 30 minutes until tender. Cool slightly, then peel; cut them in half, then cut a thin slice off the rounded end of each half so the potato will sit flat. Preheat the oven to 250°C/475°F/gas 9.

2 Meanwhile, place the butter in a frying pan and turn the heat to high. When it melts, add the cucumber and a large pinch of salt; cook for 3 minutes, shaking the pan occasionally. Add the milk and boil for 10 minutes, stirring occasionally. Add the mint and cook for 1 minute more. Leave to cool, then strain.

3 While the cucumber cooks, squeeze 2 tablespoons of juice from the grapefruit, then section the pulp.

4 Stir the yogurt, grapefruit juice, and chilli paste into the cucumber mixture; add salt to taste.

5 Mince the salmon and combine it with the shallot, oil, spinach, and salt and pepper to taste. Butter a baking tray; shape the salmon mixture into 8 balls and place on the tray. Bake for just 2 minutes; the interior of the salmon balls should remain raw.

6 To assemble, place 2 potato halves, wider side up, in each of 4 bowls. Sprinkle with a little salt, then top with a salmon ball. Spoon a portion of the cucumber milk around the potatoes, and place a few pieces of grapefruit in each bowl. Finish with a squeeze of lime and the coriander.

This is ginger ale for grown-ups; a spicy, not-too-sweet, ultra-refreshing drink that combines fresh ginger, lemongrass, and chillies in a way you've probably never had them.

MAKES ABOUT 1.25 LITRES/2 PINTS SYRUP, ENOUGH TO MAKE AT LEAST 10 GLASSES   The syrup keeps for weeks, refrigerated.

FRESH GINGER ALE WITH LEMONGRASS

500g/1lb fresh ginger, unpeeled and cut into small dice

2 stalks lemongrass, trimmed and roughly chopped

2 small fresh chillies, stems removed

375g/¾lb sugar

Soda water

Lime wedges

1 Combine the ginger, lemongrass and chillies in a food processor and process until minced, stopping the machine periodically and scraping down the sides, if necessary.

2 Place the purée in a saucepan with the sugar and 1.25l/2 pints of water. Bring to the boil over high heat, then reduce the heat to medium and simmer for about 15 minutes. Turn off the heat. Cool, then strain and chill.

3 To serve, place about 4 tablespoons of the syrup in a glass full of ice. Fill with soda water; taste and add more syrup if you like. Garnish with a lime wedge, then serve.

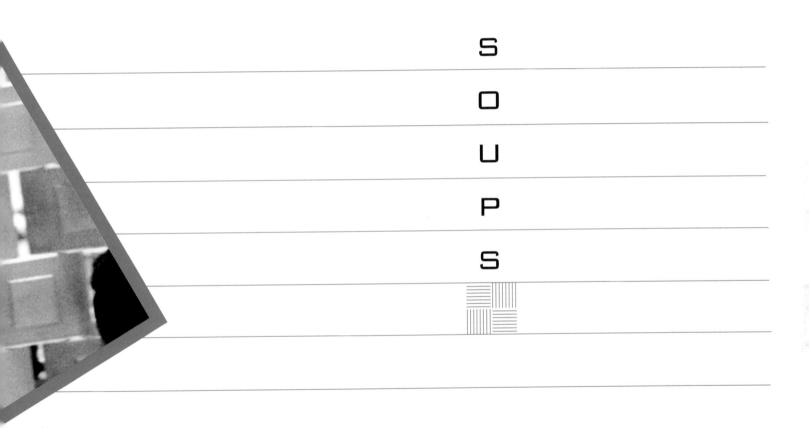

S
O
U
P
S

Jean-Georges serves this creamy, mild soup, in which garlic is used as a vegetable, without garnish. But, if you like, place a bed of chopped greens, such as watercress, arugula or parsley in the bottom of each bowl before ladling in the soup.

If you soak the garlic cloves in warm water to cover as you're working on them, the peels will slip off more easily; or blanch the separated cloves in boiling water to cover for 15 seconds or so for easier peeling.

SERVES 4

GARLIC SOUP

3 tablespoons extra virgin olive oil

4 whole garlic bulbs, separated into cloves, peeled, and thinly sliced

2 teaspoons fresh thyme leaves

1.35l/2¼ pints Rich Chicken Stock (page 195) or other stock

Salt and freshly ground black pepper

2 eggs

1 tablespoon white wine or Champagne vinegar

1 Place the olive oil in a saucepan and turn the heat to medium; immediately add the garlic and thyme. Cook, stirring occasionally, for about 10 minutes, until the garlic has a translucent appearance and begins to soften. If you taste it at this point, it will already be quite mild.

2 Add the chicken stock and bring to the boil over high heat. Reduce the heat to medium – you want the soup to be bubbling, but not furiously – and cook, stirring occasionally, until the liquid is reduced by about half and the garlic is very tender, about 15 minutes. (You may prepare the recipe in advance up to this point; refrigerate in a covered container for up to 2 days.)

3 Season the soup to taste with salt and pepper and reduce the heat as low as possible. Beat the eggs with the vinegar and gently whisk into the soup; the eggs will cook in shreds and thicken the soup. Taste and add more salt, pepper or vinegar if you like – the vinegar should make its presence felt, but not too boldly. Serve.

Here are soup-and-salad in one bowl and, because the dish uses water rather than stock, it is easy to make.

It is delicious, even when made entirely with button mushrooms.

This substantial soup may be served with a salad for a light meal.

Or, follow it with something grand, such as Gently Cooked Salmon

with Mashed Potatoes (page 78) or Sautéed Chicken with Figs

SERVES 4   (page 87).

 # MUSHROOM SOUP WITH GREENS

1kg/2lb button mushrooms, stems and all

125g/4oz shiitake mushrooms or use all button mushrooms

4 tablespoons butter

Salt

4 to 6 large shallots, roughly chopped

6 garlic cloves, lightly smashed (don't bother to peel)

4 thyme sprigs

2 tablespoons minced shallot

75g/2½oz fresh or frozen and thawed peas

2 teaspoons hazelnut or walnut oil

2 tablespoons soy sauce

Freshly cracked black pepper

1 tablespoon port

2 large handfuls mixed salad greens

2 tablespoons toasted breadcrumbs

1   Rinse the button mushrooms, then chop them coarsely. Remove the caps from the shiitakes; slice the caps and set aside. Combine the stems with the button mushrooms. (If using all button mushrooms, slice the remaining 125g/4oz mushrooms and set aside.)

2   Place 2 tablespoons butter in a deep frying pan or saucepan, turn the heat to high, and add the chopped button mushrooms and a sprinkling of salt. When the mushrooms release their liquid, add the chopped shallots, garlic, and thyme. Keep cooking over high heat, stirring and tossing occasionally, for about 5 or 10 minutes, until the mushrooms are brown. Add 1.35l/2¼ pints water. Keep the heat high to medium-high and cook at a steady, but not rolling, boil until reduced by about half, 30 minutes or so.

3   Put the mixture through a strainer, pressing hard to extract all the juices. Keep the broth warm. (You may prepare the recipe in advance up to this point; refrigerate in a covered container for up to 2 days.)

4   While the broth is cooking, place the remaining 2 tablespoons butter in a frying pan, turn the heat to high and add the minced shallot and shiitake caps (or sliced button mushrooms). Cook, stirring, until the mushrooms are tender, about 5 minutes. Add the peas and cook for 1 more minute. Turn off the heat and stir in the hazelnut oil and 1 tablespoon soy sauce.

5   Reheat the broth. Season it with the remaining soy sauce, lots of cracked pepper and the port. Taste and adjust the seasonings as necessary.

6   Place the greens in a large tureen (or in 4 individual bowls) and spoon the shiitake mixture and its juices over them. Add the breadcrumbs, pour the soup over all and serve.

A perfect winter soup with splendid colour. Jean-Georges uses an entire bunch of parsley, including the stems, making it the dominant flavour. Use any combination of mushrooms you like.

Follow the soup with something simple, such as Roast Poussins with Herb-Bread Stuffing (page 96).

SERVES 4

PARSLEY SOUP WITH MIXED MUSHROOMS

1 large bunch parsley
(100–125g/3–4oz)

2½ tablespoons butter or extra
virgin olive oil

25g/1oz minced onion

1 medium leek, trimmed, split in
half, well washed and roughly
chopped

1 medium-to-large parsnip, chopped
or substitute potato

Salt and freshly ground black pepper

600ml/1 pint Rich Chicken Stock
(page 195), Dark Chicken Stock
(page 196), or other stock;
or use all water

125g/4oz mushrooms (use an
assortment, all button mushrooms,
or button mushrooms mixed with a
tablespoon or two of reconstituted
porcini)

1 tablespoon minced shallot

1 Wash the parsley in a bowl; separate the stems and tops and tie the stems into a bundle.

2 In a casserole or large saucepan, melt half the tablespoons butter or oil over medium heat. Stir in the onion, leek, parsnip and a healthy pinch of salt. Cook, stirring occasionally, until the onion becomes translucent, about 10 minutes; do not allow the vegetables to brown. Add the parsley stems and pepper to taste and stir again.

3 Add 600ml/1 pint of water and the stock and stir. Bring to the boil over high heat, reduce the heat to medium, and cook, stirring now and then, until the vegetables are very tender, 30 to 45 minutes.

4 Meanwhile, wash and trim the mushrooms (add any undamaged stalks to the simmering soup). Chop the caps roughly. Heat the remaining butter or oil in a frying pan over medium-high heat and add the mushrooms and shallot. Season with salt and pepper and cook, stirring occasionally, until the mushrooms have given up their water and are tender, about 10 minutes. Set aside.

5 When the vegetables are soft, remove the parsley stems, add the remaining parsley, and cook for another minute. Let the soup cool slightly, if possible. Then place the soup, in batches if necessary, in a blender and purée until as smooth as possible.

6 Taste the soup and adjust the seasoning. If it seems fibrous, pass it quickly through a coarse strainer. Reheat.

7 Place a portion of mushrooms at the bottom of each of 4 bowls and top with a ladleful of the hot soup. Serve immediately.

This velvety soup is quite sweet, but cayenne lends a little bite; its bright orange colour and creamy texture make it a real crowd pleaser. You can prepare the soup with any winter squash, such as acorn or even pumpkin. Early in the season, before the squash is fully ripe, you may need to add a little sugar to the liquid. But as summer turns to autumn, there will be enough natural sweetness in the vegetable and you can eliminate the sugar altogether.

Serve it garnished, if you like, with shrimps or mushrooms, sautéed in butter or grilled with a little olive oil.

SERVES 4

CREAMY BUTTERNUT SQUASH SOUP

1kg/2lb butternut squash, peeled and cut into chunks

900ml/1½ pints Rich Chicken Stock (page 195) or other stock

300ml/½ pint sour cream, crème fraîche, or double cream

2 tablespoons butter

Salt and freshly ground black pepper

¼ teaspoon cayenne pepper, or to taste

About 1 tablespoon sugar (optional)

Sautéed or grilled shrimps or mushrooms, optional

Several chives, cut into 2.5cm/1in pieces

1 Combine the squash and stock in a saucepan and bring to the boil over high heat. Reduce the heat to medium and simmer for about 20 minutes, or until the squash is very tender.

2 Cool a bit for safety's sake, then purée the mixture in a blender. (You may prepare the recipe in advance up to this point; refrigerate in a covered container for up to 2 days.)

3 Return the purée to the saucepan and turn the heat to medium-low. Stir in the sour cream, crème fraîche, or cream, along with the butter, salt and pepper to taste, and the cayenne. Cook, stirring, until heated through (do not boil), then taste and add sugar and more seasoning, if necessary. Keep warm over low heat.

4 Serve the soup with a few cooked shrimps or mushrooms if you like, and the chives.

Like the Soup of Red Fruits (page 150) and the Asparagus with Mixed Mushrooms and Parmesan (page 124), this demonstrates Jean-Georges's uncanny ability to use, to great advantage, those food trimmings – in this case, pea pods – that most people throw out without a thought.

SERVES 4

You may make this dish with frozen peas, but it is the simmering of the pods that makes it distinctive.

# FRESH PEA SOUP

1kg/2lb peas in the shell (or 500g/1lb frozen peas)

175g/6oz butter

1 large onion, coarsely chopped

1 medium leek, trimmed, split in half, well washed and roughly chopped

3 garlic cloves, roughly chopped (don't bother to peel)

2 thyme sprigs

Salt and freshly ground black pepper

900ml/1½ pints Rich Chicken Stock (page 195) or other stock

3 tablespoons extra virgin olive oil

4 thick slices good crusty bread

1 Shell the peas, reserving all the undamaged pods and discarding those that are badly bruised or slightly rotten. Coarsely chop the pods.

2 Place 2 tablespoons of butter in a deep frying pan or broad saucepan and turn the heat to medium-high. Add the onion, leek, garlic, thyme and a sprinkling of salt and pepper. Cook for 2 or 3 minutes, stirring. When the vegetables begin to soften, add the pea pods, if using, and stir.

3 Add the stock, cover and bring to the boil. Reduce the heat to medium and cook for about 20 minutes, then strain, pressing on the vegetables to extract as much liquid as possible. (You may prepare the recipe in advance up to this point; refrigerate in a covered container for up to a day.)

4 Return the broth to a saucepan and reheat.

5 Meanwhile, blanch the peas in boiling salted water to cover until tender, 4 or 5 minutes. Drain, reserving 3 tablespoons of the cooking liquid. Take 75g/2½oz of peas and plunge them into iced water, or hold under cold running water for a minute; drain again and set aside.

6 Place the olive oil in a large frying pan and turn the heat to medium-high. Cook the bread (you can do this in batches, if necessary) in the oil until golden-brown on both sides, sprinkling it with salt as it cooks. Cut each slice of bread into large cubes or slices.

7 Place the peas in a blender with the remaining 2 tablespoons of butter, a large pinch of salt, and 2 tablespoons of the reserved pea-cooking liquid. Purée, adding the remainder of the liquid if necessary.

8 Stir the purée into the broth in 2 or 3 batches. Heat through, then taste and adjust seasoning.

9 Put some of the bread in each of 4 bowls, then spoon in the soup and a portion of the reserved peas.

PEA SOUP WITH VEGETABLES

You can make this soup even more substantial with the addition of vegetables. Dice 1 trimmed medium leek and about 125g/4oz peeled celeriac (or 1 celery stalk) into cubes 5mm/¼in or smaller on each side. Place 2 tablespoons of extra virgin olive oil in a frying pan and turn the heat to high. Add the vegetables and a pinch of salt and cook, stirring frequently, until tender, 5 to 10 minutes. Add to the soup along with the bread and peas.

A more-or-less traditional Thai dish that has been on the Vong menu since its opening, this combines bright flavours and a lovely combination of colours – the soup is yellow, with brown shiitake, white chicken and bright green coriander peeking through the broth.

The base of this can be prepared in advance and, in fact, tastes better when it is done a day ahead. To turn into a main course, increase the amount of chicken to 500g/1lb or more, and serve with white rice, which can be eaten on the side or spooned into the soup. For a real feast, use Sticky Rice Steamed in Banana Leaves (page 145).

SERVES 4

CHICKEN SOUP WITH COCONUT MILK AND LEMONGRASS

1 stalk lemongrass

1 tablespoon vegetable, grapeseed or other neutral-flavoured oil

1 medium onion, minced

1 garlic clove, minced

2 teaspoons Thai red curry paste or curry powder

Six 3mm/⅛in-thick slices galangal or ginger, not peeled

3 lime leaves, dried or fresh

900ml/1½ pints Rich Chicken Stock (page 195) or other stock

375g/¾lb boneless, skinless chicken breast

250g/½lb shiitake mushrooms

One 400-ml/14-fl oz can unsweetened coconut milk

Juice of 2 limes

2 tablespoons nam pla or nuoc mam (Asian fish sauce)

3 spring onions, trimmed and minced

4–6 sprigs minced coriander

1 Trim the lemongrass of its outer sheath and hard ends, whack it in a few places with the back of a knife, then cut it into 2 or 3 pieces. In a deep frying pan or medium saucepan, combine the oil, onion and garlic and turn the heat to medium. Cook for a minute, stirring, then add the lemongrass, curry paste, galangal or ginger and lime leaves.

2 Cook, stirring, for 3 or 4 minutes, then add the stock. Bring to the boil, then reduce the heat to medium, and cook at a moderate boil for about 15 minutes. (You may prepare the recipe in advance up to this point; refrigerate in a covered container for up to 2 days.)

3 While the broth cooks, cut the chicken breast into 3–4cm/½–¾in cubes. Remove the stems from the shiitakes and discard or reserve for stock; cut the caps into quarters or eighths.

4 Add the coconut milk, then the chicken and the mushrooms to the broth. Cook for about 5 minutes, or until the chicken is done.

5 Stir in the lime juice and nam pla; taste and adjust the seasoning. Divide among 4 bowls, then garnish with the spring onions and coriander and serve. You may remove the galangal and lemongrass before serving, or leave them in; they are delicious to gnaw on at the table.

Not a gazpacho, but a fresh-tasting tomato purée with an unusual but simple garnish. Make it with good summer tomatoes and you'll find it hard to get enough of this. To make the dish more elaborate, add some shredded crab or minced cooked shrimps along with the cucumber.

For a light lunch, serve this with any salad; for a more substantial meal, follow it with Monkfish with Almonds and Spices (page 77) or Salmon and Potato Crisps (page 80).

SERVES 4

COLD TOMATO SOUP WITH CUCUMBER AND CANTALOUPE

1kg/2lb tomatoes

2 garlic cloves, minced

6 basil leaves

4 tablespoons extra virgin olive oil

2 tablespoons red wine vinegar

1/4 teaspoon sugar

Salt and plenty of freshly ground black pepper

1 cucumber, peeled, halved and deseeded

Cantaloupe, watermelon and/or honeydew

Chopped fresh basil

1 Core the tomatoes and chop them roughly, combining them in a saucepan with their seeds and juice, together with the garlic, basil leaves, oil, vinegar, sugar, a big pinch of salt and about 1/4 teaspoon black pepper. Heat to about 65°C/150°F – hot, but well below boiling point.

2 Remove from the heat and strain through a not-too-fine sieve, just to remove the seeds and skins. Cool either over a bowl of ice water (if you're in a hurry) or in the refrigerator (if you're not). Taste and adjust the seasoning as necessary.

3 When you're ready to eat, use the small end of a melon baller to scoop about 40 tiny balls from the cucumber and melons. (You may also simply dice the cucumber and the melons.) Divide the cucumber and melon balls among 4 bowls and pour the soup over them; garnish with the chopped basil and serve.

Spiked with chillies, nam pla and lime, this is a far cry from the usual sour-cream-and-dill cucumber soup, and a welcome change in midsummer. It may be prepared a day or two in advance, and can be made more substantial by adding about a cup of cold cooked crab-meat or shrimps at the last minute.

Follow this soup with Chicken with Lemongrass (page 90) or 9-Spice Rack of Lamb with Cucumber Relish (page 115).

SERVES 4

SPICY COLD CUCUMBER SOUP

About 2kg/4lb cucumbers

2 small fresh chillies, minced, or dried red pepper flakes to taste

2 tablespoons nam pla or nuoc mam (Asian fish sauce), or salt to taste

Juice of 3 limes

1 tablespoon chopped mint leaves

1 tablespoon chopped coriander leaves

250g/8oz cooked crabmeat or shrimp chunks (optional)

1 Wash the cucumbers, but don't peel them. Cut off a piece of one and mince enough to make 175g/6oz; set aside. Put the rest of the cucumbers through a juicer, or purée in a blender or food processor and wring the resulting pulp in a cheesecloth to extract the juice.

2 Season the juice with the chillies, nam pla, and lime juice. Chill well. (You may prepare the recipe in advance up to this point; refrigerate in a covered container for up to 2 days.)

3 Taste the soup and adjust the seasoning, if necessary. Serve, garnished with the reserved minced cucumber, mint, coriander, and crabmeat or shrimps, if using.

S
I
M
P
L
E

G
O
O
D

F
O
O
D

34

TOMATO TOWER WITH BASIL

COUNTER-CLOCKWISE:

BEETROOT AND GINGER SALAD,

BEETROOT RAVIOLI WITH BEETROOT

SAUCE, CARAMELISED BEETROOTS

AND TURNIPS, BEETROOT TARTARE

COUNTER-CLOCKWISE:

FENNEL AND APPLE SALAD WITH

JUNIPER, WATERMELON-GOAT'S

CHEESE SALAD, SIMPLY THE BEST

CRAB SALAD WITH CUMIN CRISPS

SCALLOPS AND CAULIFLOWER

WITH CAPER-RAISIN SAUCE

CURRIED MUSSELS

RED SNAPPER WITH TOMATO

CONFIT AND TAPENADE

SAUTÉED CHICKEN WITH GREEN OLIVES

AND CORIANDER SIMMERED CARROTS

WITH CUMIN AND ORANGE

DUCK À LA JOJO WITH MILLET CAKE

This refreshing concoction only gets better if you refrigerate it for a day or two before serving, and you can't make soup any faster than this. If the ice cubes are large, crush them before putting them in the blender – just put them in a heavy plastic bag and whack the bag a few times with a rolling pin or the bottom of a heavy pot.

This technique will work with any tender green: Jean-Georges uses lamb's-lettuce – sold in supermarkets now – when he can get it, spinach when he cannot.

SERVES 4

10-MINUTE GREEN GAZPACHO

1 slice Italian or French bread (about 15g/½oz), trimmed of crusts and torn into pieces

250–300g/8–10oz spinach, lamb's lettuce, or other tender cooking greens, trimmed of thick stems

4 tablespoons vegetable, grapeseed or other neutral-flavoured oil

About 150g/5oz small ice cubes

Salt

Cayenne pepper

Tabasco pepper sauce

1 Bring a medium pot of salted water to the boil. Soak the bread in cold water to cover while you prepare the greens.

2 Plunge the greens into the boiling water. When the water returns to the boil, cook for 30 seconds. Drain and plunge them into a bowl of iced water to stop the cooking; drain again.

3 Squeeze the bread to remove excess water. Place the bread, cooked greens, oil and ice cubes in a blender and process until very smooth; add a couple of tablespoons of water, if necessary, to get the machine going.

4 Season the soup with salt, cayenne and Tabasco to taste. Serve immediately, or store in a covered container in the refrigerator for a day or two before eating.

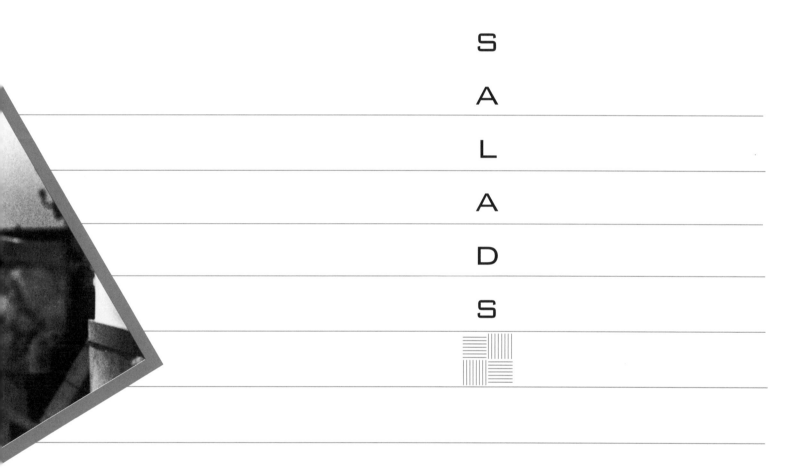

S
A
L
A
D
S

Cold rice noodles are tossed with grapefruit, peanuts, vegetables, herbs and spices. While the whole is greater than the sum of its parts, the individual flavours somehow remain distinct. It's bright and refreshing, a perfect summer lunch, and an unusual one.

SERVES 4 TO 6 — This salad is almost as good without the shrimps.

SHRIMP AND NOODLE SALAD
WITH GRAPEFRUIT AND PEANUTS

250g/8oz rice vermicelli

1 stalk lemongrass

1 large grapefruit, peeled, sectioned and chopped

50g/2oz chopped peanuts

1 medium-to-large ripe tomato, peeled, deseeded and chopped

3 spring onions, white and green, minced

1 handful coarsely chopped mint leaves

1 large handful coarsely chopped coriander leaves

1 or 2 small fresh chillies, minced, or about 1 teaspoon dried red chilli flakes, or to taste

1 garlic clove, finely minced

1 packed tablespoon brown or palm sugar

Juice of 5 limes

2 tablespoons nam pla or nuoc mam (Asian fish sauce)

24 medium-to-large shrimps, peeled

1 tablespoon peanut or other oil

Salt and freshly ground black pepper

1 Soak the rice noodles in fairly hot water (about 50°C/120°F, almost too hot to touch) for 10 to 20 minutes, or until soft. Meanwhile, set a large pot of water to boil. Trim the stalk of lemongrass, and peel off enough layers to expose its tender core. Finely mince enough to make about 1 tablespoon.

2 Mix together the grapefruit, 40g/1½oz peanuts, tomato, spring onions, mint, ⅔ of the coriander, and the lemongrass in a large bowl.

3 In a small bowl, combine the chillies, garlic, sugar, lime juice and nam pla. Taste and adjust the seasoning. (This dressing may be prepared a day or two in advance; its flavour will improve on standing.)

4 Drain the noodles and plunge them into the boiling water. When the water returns to the boil, drain the noodles and rinse them in two or three changes of cold water. Drain well, then toss in the large bowl with the grapefruit mixture and the dressing.

5 Brush the shrimps with the oil and sauté or grill them for 2 minutes per side, or until done; season with a little salt and pepper. Place the shrimps on top of the noodles, then garnish with remaining coriander and chopped peanuts, and serve.

S
I
M
P
L
E

G
O
O
D

F
O
O
D

An ideal summer lunch or supper dish served throughout the season at JoJo – just filling enough, but light, refreshing, and full of flavour.

Use whatever mix of herbs you can find, balancing more of the lighter ones (chervil, parsley, basil, mint and dill) with fewer of the stronger ones (chives, tarragon, sage, lavender and rosemary). In any case, do not mince the herbs – they should be just chopped or, in the case of thyme leaves, left whole (the tarragon leaf is the exception).

SERVES 4

CHICKEN AND HERB SALAD WITH RED PEPPER OIL

1 teaspoon thyme leaves

50g/2oz mixed coarsely chopped chervil, basil, dill and parsley

1 tablespoon minced chives

1 tarragon leaf, minced

4 handfuls mixed salad greens

Juice of 2 lemons

3 red capsicum peppers

4 tablespoons extra virgin olive oil

Salt and freshly ground black pepper

4 boneless, skinless chicken cutlets (about 500g/1lb)

1 Preheat the oven to 230°C/450°F/gas 8. Mix the herbs together. Place the mixed salad greens on a platter.

2 Marinate about ³/₄ of the herb mixture in the lemon juice while you prepare the peppers and chicken.

3 If you have a juicer, juice the peppers. If not, stem and deseed them, then purée them in a food processor, scraping down the mixture occasionally. Squeeze the purée in a cheesecloth to extract all the juice. Cook the juice in a small saucepan over medium-high heat until it is syrupy and reduced to about 2 tablespoons, about 15 minutes. Stir in 3 tablespoons of the olive oil, along with salt and pepper to taste. The mixture will be sweet, with a tiny bit of heat in the finish.

4 Drain the herbs, reserving the lemon juice. Heat the remaining 2 tablespoons of olive oil in an ovenproof frying pan over medium-high heat, then cook the chicken for 3 minutes on one side; it will barely begin to brown. Turn the chicken over, top with the drained herb mixture and transfer it to the oven for 5 more minutes, or until it is cooked through.

5 When the chicken is done, drizzle it with the reserved lemon juice. Top the mixed greens with the chicken and its pan juices, then sprinkle all with the remaining herbs. Drizzle the red pepper juice around the edges of the platter and serve.

'When I was working in Bangkok, I wanted to make an interesting salad that was both hot and cold,' says Jean-Georges. So successful is this salad – asparagus, avocado, mushrooms, and greens, with not one, but two, luxurious dressings explain why – that it has been on almost every menu he's developed in the last fifteen years. Although it's a little bit of a big deal – largely because of the presence of the truffle juice and the necessity of making a quick hollandaise sauce – the first of these challenges can be ignored (see Note) and the second is a simple 5-minute process. You should try this salad; it's truly unforgettable.

Note that the asparagus must be cooked at the last minute, even after making the hollandaise – the contrast between hot and cold is part of the magic here. The hollandaise will hold perfectly if you keep it warm, and can even be reheated gently within a half hour or so of making it.

This is big and filling, so either serve it as a light meal, or follow it with something quite simple, such as Dill-Stuffed Shrimps with Baked Lemon (page 63).

SERVES 4–6

ASPARAGUS SALAD WITH SOY VINAIGRETTE AND HOLLANDAISE

2 tablespoons truffle juice

2 tablespoons soy sauce

2 tablespoons lemon juice

5 tablespoons extra virgin olive oil

¼ teaspoon freshly ground black pepper

6 handfuls mesclun or other salad greens

2 large or extra-large egg yolks

Salt

25g/1oz butter, softened

1 To make the soy vinaigrette, combine the truffle juice, soy sauce, 1½ table-spoons of lemon juice, the oil and black pepper. Whisk until smooth; set aside. (This dressing will keep well, covered and refrigerated, for days.)

2 Bring a pot of salted water to the boil. Divide the mesclun among 4 plates.

3 To make the hollandaise, place the yolks in a small saucepan or top of a double-boiler and add 2 tablespoons water and a pinch of salt; place over hot water or extremely low heat, whisking constantly, until light, foamy, and slightly thickened. (If at any point during this process the yolks begin to cur-dle, immediately remove the pot from the heat and continue to whisk for a minute before returning the pot to the stove.) Remove from the heat and stir in the butter. Return to the heat and continue to whisk until the mixture is thick and bright yellow. Add 1 teaspoon lemon juice. Keep this in a warm place – on the side of the stove, or over some very hot water – and whisk it occasionally while you prepare the rest of the salad.

1 ripe avocado, cut into four, peeled and sliced thinly

4 large button mushrooms, destemmed, peeled and roughly chopped

12 large asparagus (about 500g/1lb), bottoms broken off (and discarded), peeled

Minced chives

4 Top the mesclun with the avocado and mushrooms and sprinkle with salt. Place the asparagus in the boiling water and cook until tender, for about 5 minutes. While it is cooking, spoon the soy dressing over the salads.

5 When the asparagus is tender, drain it and immediately lay it over the mushrooms. Nap with the hollandaise, garnish with the chives, and serve.

NOTE:

Truffle juice is a rare, expensive ingredient that is a much subtler representation of the flavour and aroma of truffles than the more common truffle oil. If you don't wish to buy it, you can make the dressing in either of these proportions:

3 tablespoons lemon juice
3 tablespoons soy sauce
5 tablespoons extra virgin olive oil
1 tablespoon truffle oil
or
3 tablespoons lemon juice
3 tablespoons soy sauce
5 tablespoons extra virgin olive oil
1 tablespoon water

As wonderful as the truffle flavour is, in fact it is soy that dominates this dressing. It's better with the truffle juice, yes, but it would be a shame to not make this wonderful salad for lack of it.

The combination of sweet beetroot, piercing ginger and woody, sour sherry vinegar is memorable. Baking beetroots tenderises them without allowing them to become waterlogged. You can steam or boil them, too, but keep the skins on and don't poke them too much.

If possible, allow the salad to sit at room temperature for 30 to 60 minutes before serving; the ginger flavour will become more pronounced.

Serve this with anything grilled; it is cool and strong, so you can't go wrong. And parents, note: this is the first beetroot preparation my kids ever relished; they now beg me to make it.

MAKES 2 LARGE OR
4 SMALL PORTIONS

 # BEETROOT AND GINGER SALAD

4 medium beetroots, about 500g/1lb

1¹/₂ tablespoons vegetable, grapeseed or other neutral-flavoured oil

2 tablespoons sherry vinegar

2 teaspoons minced ginger

Salt and freshly ground black pepper

3 or 4 chives cut into 5cm/2in sections, optional

1 To bake the beetroots, preheat the oven to 180°C/350°F/gas 4. Wash the beetroots, leave them wet, and wrap them individually in foil. Place them in a roasting pan or on a baking tray and bake for about 90 minutes, or until they're nice and tender (poke a thin-bladed knife right through the foil to test). Leave to cool in the foil. (To cook in water, just drop them into salted water to cover, bring to the boil, and cook over medium heat until tender; it will take less time – 45 to 60 minutes.)

2 Peel the beetroots and cut them into disks, cubes or thin strips. Mix together the oil, vinegar, ginger and salt and pepper to taste in a bowl, then toss with the beetroots. Allow to rest for about 30 minutes before serving, if you have the time. (This recipe keeps well for up to 1 day; refrigerate in a covered container and bring to room temperature before serving.)

3 Garnish with chives, if desired, and serve.

Not a misprint, and far more than a play on words, since you will prefer these highly seasoned beetroots to raw beef. This salad keeps very well and makes a wonderful picnic dish. If possible, stir in the mayonnaise and make the seasoning adjustments at the last minute.

Jean-Georges, who developed this to use the flavours of beef tartare in a vegetarian dish, serves this as an accompaniment to fish dishes – such as Halibut Steaks with Mixed Vegetables (page 73) – but it can also work as a pre-dinner dip with raw vegetables.

MAKES 4 SERVINGS

BEETROOT TARTARE

6 medium beetroots (about 625g/1¼lb)

1 shallot, roughly chopped

1 teaspoon Worcestershire sauce

Few drops Tabasco or other hot pepper sauce

1 teaspoon sherry vinegar

6 cornichons, roughly chopped

2 tablespoons capers, drained

1 tablespoon mayonnaise

2 tablespoons chopped parsley, plus more for garnish

Salt and freshly ground black pepper (optional)

1 To bake the beetroot, preheat the oven to 180°C/350°F/gas 4. Wash the beetroot, leave them wet and wrap them individually in foil. Place them in a roasting pan or on a baking sheet and bake for about 90 minutes, or until they're nice and tender (poke a thin-bladed knife right through the foil to test). Leave to cool in the foil. (To cook in water, just drop them into salted water to cover, bring to the boil, and cook over medium heat until tender; it will take less time – 45 to 60 minutes.)

2 Cool the beetroots, peel, then cut them into eighths.

3 Place the beetroots in a food processor with the shallot, Worcestershire sauce, Tabasco, vinegar, cornichons and capers. Pulse until the mixture is minced but not puréed. You may need to scrape down the mixture between pulses.

4 Spoon the mixture into a bowl and stir in the mayonnaise and 2 tablespoons of parsley. Taste and adjust seasonings: you may need to add salt, pepper, more vinegar, or a little more Worcestershire or Tabasco sauce. (This recipe keeps well for up to 2 days; refrigerate in a covered container and bring to room temperature before serving.)

5 Garnish with additional parsley and serve.

I love this as a salad – it's lightning quick, stunningly flavourful, and fat-free. Or, use it as a bed under grilled swordfish, tuna or chicken, or for Soft-Shell Crabs Tempura (see page 58, omitting the passionfruit sauce).

We've made this with savoy cabbage, with Napa cabbage, and plain old green cabbage. More important than the type of cabbage is using cracked coriander seeds rather than powdered coriander – it's more flavourful, and the crunchy texture delightful.

SERVES 4

SAVOY COLESLAW WITH CITRUS, GINGER AND MUSTARD

1 tablespoon yellow mustard powder

1 tablespoon sugar

1 teaspoon grated or minced lemon zest

1 teaspoon grated or minced orange zest

1 teaspoon grated or minced ginge

50ml/2fl oz rice or other mild vinegar

Salt and freshly ground black pepper

1 teaspoon crushed coriander seeds

1 teaspoon honey

1 small head savoy, white or other cabbage, or half of a larger head

1 In a small bowl, mix together the mustard, sugar and 1 tablespoon of water. Stir to blend and set aside.

2 In a large bowl, mix together the zests, ginger, vinegar, salt and pepper to taste, coriander and honey. Stir well to blend all the ingredients.

3 In a food processor, with a grater or with a knife, shred enough cabbage to make 225g/7oz. Toss in the bowl with the flavourings. (You may prepare the recipe in advance up to this point. Refrigerate in a covered container for up to 1 day; return to room temperature before serving.)

4 To serve, place a portion of the coleslaw on each plate and drizzle with a little of the mustard mixture.

This salad was developed to be served with Marinated Quail, Vong-Style (page 103), but it can certainly stand on its own. You might be tempted to make it without frying the leeks – the only serious work involved – but their contrasting sweet crunch is what makes this dish unique.

SERVES 4

If you have a mandoline, use it to shave the leeks and shred the cabbage; it makes quick work of both.

RED CABBAGE AND WATERCRESS SALAD

2 leeks, white part only, well washed

4 tabelspoons vegetable, grapeseed or other neutral-flavoured oil

Salt

1 bunch watercress, thick stems removed

150g/5oz finely shredded or julienned red cabbage

1½ tablespoons soy sauce

1 tablespoon hazelnut, walnut or olive oil

1 tablespoon minced shallot

1 tablespoon sherry vinegar

Freshly ground black pepper

Chopped chives

1 Cut the leeks into fine rings or julienne, using a mandoline if you have one. Place the oil in a frying pan and turn the heat to medium. Add half the leeks and cook, stirring. When they are golden to brown, remove them immediately with a slotted spoon; be careful – once they start to brown they brown quickly. Drain on kitchen roll and repeat the process. Sprinkle with salt. These will stay crisp for a few days in a covered container (do not refrigerate), so make extra if you like.

2 Toss together the watercress and cabbage.

3 Combine the soy sauce, oil, shallot, vinegar and pepper. Toss the dressing and most of the leeks with the watercress and cabbage mixture. Taste and add salt if necessary, then top with the remaining leeks. Garnish with chopped chives and serve.

Developed by Vong chef Pierre Schutz, this salad is unusual not only for its basic flavours, which are decidedly Vietnamese, but for the fact that it is overdressed, then drained of extra dressing, which makes it wilted and juicy. The infusions can sit for hours if you like, but the salad must be assembled at the last minute or it will become soggy.

This makes a terrific counterpart to any browned meat, such as 9-Spice Rack of Lamb with Cucumber Relish (page 115).

SERVES 4

CUCUMBER SALAD WITH LEMONGRASS

125ml/4fl oz white vinegar

1 Thai chilli, very finely minced

1 garlic clove, very finely minced

2 stalks lemongrass

400g/14oz thinly sliced cucumber

25g/1oz bean sprouts

125g/4oz cubed jicama, apple or Asian pear

125g/4oz shredded carrot

25g/1oz minced mint and coriander, mixed

1 tablespoon nam pla or nuoc mam (Asian fish sauce)

1 tablespoon vegetable, grapeseed or other neutral-flavoured oil

15 roughly chopped mint leaves, plus more for garnish

4–6 sprigs roughly chopped coriander leaves, plus more for garnish

1 Combine the vinegar, chilli and garlic in a small saucepan and bring to the boil. Cover and let cool while you prepare the other ingredients.

2 Trim one stalk of lemongrass and chop it roughly. Place it in a saucepan with 125ml/4fl oz of water, cover, and bring to the boil. Turn off the heat and leave to cool.

3 Trim the other stalk of lemongrass, then peel off enough layers to expose its tender core. Finely mince enough to make about 1 tablespoon.

4 Combine the cucumber, bean sprouts, jicama, carrot, minced mint and coriander, nam pla, oil and the roughly chopped mint leaves and coriander in a bowl. Add the minced lemongrass, the cooled vinegar, and 4 tablespoons of the lemongrass water. Toss together, leave to rest for a minute, then remove to another bowl with a slotted spoon. Garnish with chopped mint and coriander leaves and serve.

In this typically unlikely combination, Jean-Georges combines two bitter ingredients – endives and black olives – then softens them by adding sour cream. The result is refreshing, even soothing (thanks to the olives, it's also slightly purple).

This salad should be eaten within 15 minutes or so of making; it does not keep well at all.

ENDIVE AND BLACK OLIVE SALAD

4 large Belgian endives (at least 375g/¾lb total)

1 tablespoon lemon juice

1 large shallot, minced

15 black olives, such as Niçoise, pitted and minced

2½ tablespoons sour cream

Salt and freshly ground black pepper

Chopped chives (optional)

1 Wipe the endives clean, then trim off the bottom 2.5cm/1in and discard. Remove the first layer of leaves. Cut in half, lengthwise, then slice thinly. (This task is made easier with a mandoline.)

2 Toss the endives in a bowl with the lemon juice, shallot and olives, reserving a tablespoon or so of olives for garnish. Stir in the sour cream. Taste and add salt, if necessary, and pepper, if you like. Serve immediately, garnished with the reserved olives and the chives, if using.

Here is one of those incredibly simple flavour combinations that Jean-Georges revels in discovering.

Serve it with grilled shrimps or smoked salmon (or eat it standing next to the refrigerator, bowl and fork in hand). If you have a mandoline, use it here.

FENNEL AND APPLE SALAD WITH JUNIPER

1 fennel bulb (about 375g/¾lb)

1 Granny Smith apple

Juice of 1 lemon

2 tablespoons extra virgin olive oil

Salt and freshly ground black pepper

15 juniper berries

1 Trim the fennel, but keep some of the top feathery fronds for garnishing. Cut the apple into quarters and core it (do not peel).

2 Cut the fennel against the grain, preferably on a mandoline, as thinly as you can. Cut the apple into the thinnest possible slices as well. Toss them both together with the lemon juice, olive oil, salt and pepper.

3 Crush the juniper berries with the side of a knife and then mince them. Stir into the salad, toss, and leave to sit for 5 minutes before serving. (This recipe keeps well for up to a day; refrigerate in a covered container and bring to room temperature before garnishing and serving.)

4 Just before serving, garnish with the minced feathery fennel tops.

An extremely light (the mushrooms are cooked in water), sweet-and-sour appetiser developed by JoJo chef Chris Beicher, which can be made entirely with mushrooms found in most supermarkets, such as oysters, shiitakes and creminis.

Better, of course, would be some chanterelles, porcini and/or morels in the mix. Note that this salad must sit for quite a while before serving. Serve with good crusty bread.

SERVES 4

MUSHROOM SALAD WITH CIDER VINEGAR AND CORIANDER

500g/1lb assorted mushrooms, trimmed (discard shiitake stems or reserve them for stock)

125ml/4fl oz extra virgin olive oil

2 big shallots, thinly sliced

2 garlic cloves, thinly sliced

1 teaspoon coriander seeds

1/2 teaspoon coarsely cracked black pepper (set your mill on the coarsest grind, or crush the peppercorns with the side of a broad-bladed knife, then mince them)

40g/1 1/2oz raisins or currants

125ml/4fl oz cider vinegar

Salt

Minced chives

1 Bring a large pot of water to the boil. If the mushrooms are not of uniform size, cut the larger ones up so they are about the same size as the smaller ones. Place them in the boiling water and cook for 2 minutes. Drain, then rinse in cold water; drain again. Place in a serving bowl and set aside.

2 Place the olive oil in a large frying pan; turn the heat to medium-high and add the shallots and garlic. Cook for 2 minutes, then reduce the heat to medium-low. Add the coriander, pepper and raisins or currants. Cook stirring, for about a minute.

3 Add the cider vinegar and salt to taste. Pour this mixture, hot, over the mushrooms, stir, and cover with foil. Leave to marinate at room temperature for at least 3 hours, and preferably overnight.

4 Serve at room temperature, garnished with chives.

A potato salad with some crunch. Be sure to save the oil in which you cook the shallots; it is wonderful for sautéing chicken breasts.

SERVES 4

Serve this with Poussins with Onion Compôte (page 98), any other poultry dish, or good hamburgers.

WARM POTATO SALAD WITH CARAMELIZED SHALLOTS AND WATERCRESS

500g/1lb small new potatoes

8 tabelspoons plus 3 tablespoons vegetable, grapeseed or other neutral-flavoured oil

6 to 8 large shallots (about 175g/6oz), thinly sliced (or use onions or leeks)

Salt

2 tablespoons grainy mustard

2 tablespoons sherry vinegar

1 tablespoon chopped chives

Freshly ground black pepper

3 to 4 bunches watercress

1 Place the potatoes in salted water to cover and bring to the boil. Reduce the heat and simmer for 15 to 30 minutes until tender, depending on their size. When they are tender, drain and peel them as soon as they are cool enough to handle. Cut into 5mm/¼in slices and place in a bowl.

2 Meanwhile, place 8 tablespoons of oil in a saucepan or deep frying pan and turn the heat to medium-high. A minute later, add the shallots and cook, stirring, until they begin to darken; this will take about 15 minutes. When they are nearly done, they will begin to brown more quickly, so be careful not to burn them. As soon as they turn golden brown, the colour of onion rings, turn off the heat and remove them with a slotted spoon. Blot them dry with two sets of kitchen roll and sprinkle them with salt. Reserve the oil for another use.

3 Mix together the mustard, vinegar and remaining 3 tablespoons of oil. Toss this with the potatoes, chives and salt and pepper to taste. Place the potatoes on top of a bed of watercress, top them with the shallots and serve.

'This is the kind of dish I make for myself,' says Jean-Georges. It's a fine lunch dish, with the sharpness of the Gorgonzola and the garlicky vinaigrette tempered by the blandness of the potatoes.

If you can, use a variety of potatoes (purple, yellow, and white) for a great presentation, and feel free to use Roquefort, Stilton, or any other mature, creamy blue in place of the Gorgonzola.

SERVES 4

 # POTATO AND MESCLUN SALAD WITH GORGONZOLA

500g/1lb waxy potatoes

About 200g/7oz mesclun

Salt and freshly ground black pepper

125g/4oz ripe but cold gorgonzola, cut into 1.2cm/½in chunks

1 recipe Honey-Garlic Vinaigrette (page 209), or other vinaigrette

Several chives, cut into 2.5cm/1in lengths (optional)

1 Place the potatoes in salted water to cover and bring to the boil. Reduce the heat and simmer for 15 to 30 minutes, until tender, depending on their size.

2 When the potatoes are tender, drain and peel them as soon as they are cool enough to handle. Cut into 5mm/¼in slices.

3 Cover the greens with the warm or room-temperature potatoes, then sprinkle with salt and pepper. Top with the gorgonzola, then spoon the vinaigrette over all. Garnish with the chives, if desired, and serve.

An unusual use for watermelon: this occurred to Jean-Georges on a visit to Hong Kong, where he saw people eating watermelon dipped in salt.

It's a supremely versatile first course; you can serve this salad before almost anything.

WATERMELON–GOAT'S CHEESE SALAD

500g/1lb wedge of watermelon, weighed after removing the rind

Coarse sea salt

250g/½lb fresh goat's cheese

About 12 white or black peppercorns

2½ tablespoons extra virgin olive oil

1 Cut the watermelon into 16 thin wedges. Divide them among 4 plates and sprinkle them with salt.

2 Crumble the goat's cheese over the melon.

3 Crack the pepper with the side of a knife or the bottom of a pot and mince it with a knife; or crush it in a mortar and pestle. It should not be too fine.

4 Sprinkle the melon and cheese with the oil and pepper and serve.

First of all: a crab salad without mayo. The crab is tossed with a classic fresh-tasting sauce called *Tomate à la Française* (which, incidentally, is great with any cold fish and makes a fine dip for vegetables or crackers).

Jean-Georges serves this at both JoJo and Jean-Georges with Cumin Crisps and Mustard Butter, but you could go with simple bread and butter. In any case, use a good ripe mango, which complements the crab perfectly.

SERVES 4

SIMPLY THE BEST CRAB SALAD

1 garlic clove

1 shallot

1 medium tomato, peeled, deseeded and cut into chunks

About 5 large basil leaves

2½ tablespoons extra virgin olive oil

2 tablespoons sherry vinegar

Salt and freshly ground black pepper

500g/1lb crab, picked-over

1 mango, peeled and cubed

Cumin Crisps (page 54) and Mustard Butter (page 212) or bread and butter

1 Combine the garlic, shallot, tomato, basil, oil and vinegar in a blender and purée. Add salt and pepper to taste. You may set this dressing aside for 2 or 3 days before using it.

2 Add enough of the dressing to the crab to moisten it (you will probably not need all of it; use the rest within a day or two as a salad dressing). Taste and correct the seasoning, if necessary. (You may prepare the recipe in advance up to this point; refrigerate in a covered container for up to 1 day.)

3 Serve the crab with the mango, and with Cumin Crisps and Mustard Butter or bread and butter.

This light sweet-and-sour batter produces a thin, crisp cracker unlike any you've ever had.

Perfect with Simply the Best Crab Salad (page 53) or any light appetiser.

MAKES ABOUT 30

CUMIN CRISPS

115g/4oz flour

2 tablespoons sugar

5 tablespoons white vinegar

1 tablespoon cumin seeds

25g/1oz butter, melted

1 Preheat the oven to 230°C/450°F/gas 8. Combine the flour and sugar in a bowl, then whisk in the vinegar until smooth. The mixture will be quite thick. Stir in the cumin seeds and butter and whisk again, then stir in enough water to make a smooth, spreadable mixture. Leave to rest for 10 minutes.

2 Brush the mixture in any shape you like onto a non-stick baking tray. (If the batter is too thick to brush, add a little more water to the mixture.) The crackers should be very thin – do not be tempted to layer the batter.

3 Bake for about 5 minutes, or until light brown. Cool (they will crisp up as they do so), remove from the tray and serve immediately, or store in a covered container for a few days.

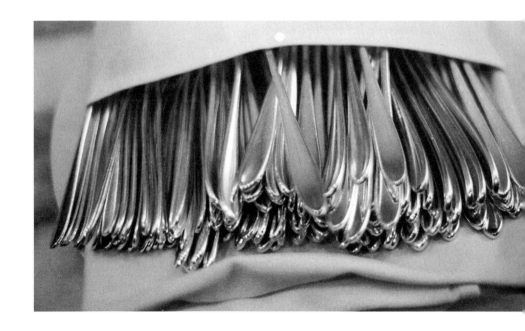

With nothing more than the addition of water, you can turn a handful of olives into a wonderfully smooth and flavourful purée. Add a few pinches of Moroccan spices, as Jean-Georges does, and the simple tapenade becomes exotic.

To use this same sauce as a dip, just add less water and the mixture will remain thick.

SERVES 4

ARUGULA SALAD WITH MOROCCAN TAPENADE

¼ teaspoon cumin seeds

¼ teaspoon cardamom pods

¼ teaspoon coriander seeds

1.2cm/½in piece cinnamon stick

150g/6oz pitted Niçoise or other good black olives

Salt and freshly ground pepper

4–6 handfuls arugula or other salad greens, washed and dried

1 Toast the cumin, cardamom, coriander and cinnamon over medium-high heat in a dry frying pan until aromatic, for about 2 minutes. Grind finely in a spice or coffee grinder.

2 Place the olives in a blender or food processor with about 8 tablespoons water and turn the machine on. With the machine running, add water in a thin stream until the mixture is coarsely ground. (You'll probably use a little more than 250ml/9fl oz of water).

3 Season the tapenade with the spice mix and add salt and pepper as necessary. Toss with the greens and serve.

FISH

AND

FISH AND SHELLFISH

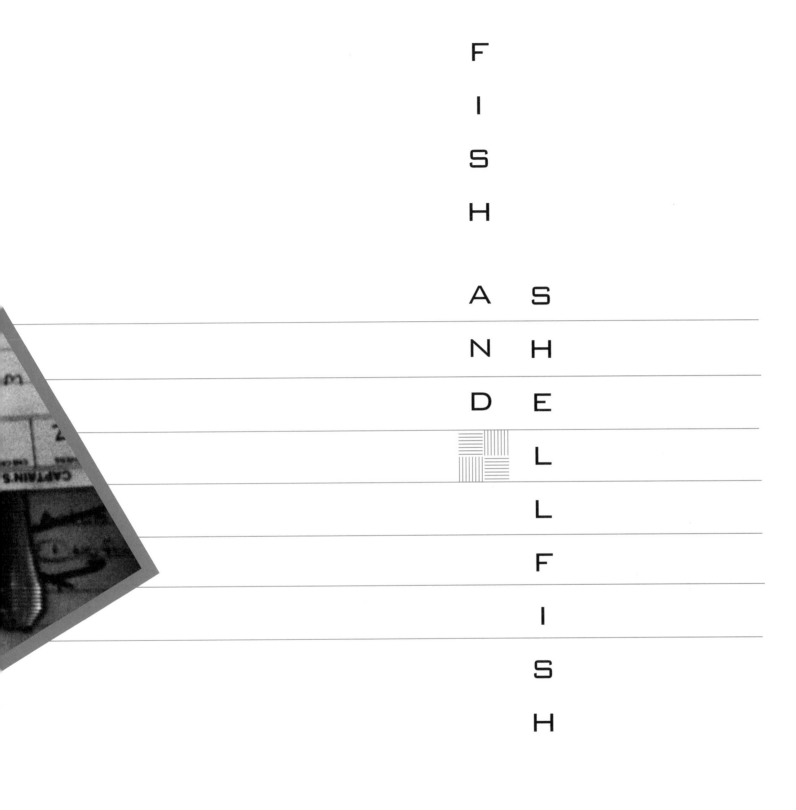

Serve these crunchy crabs with the passionfruit sauce (below) or on a bed of Savoy Coleslaw with Citrus, Ginger and Mustard (page 44; drizzle the mustard sauce over the crabs *and* the salad).

SERVES 4

Note that you must use iced water for the tempura batter and that the batter must remain very lumpy to ensure crisp fried crabs.

SOFT-SHELL CRABS TEMPURA

4 tablespoons butter

125ml/4fl oz bottled or canned passionfruit juice

Salt and freshly ground black pepper

1 tablespoon lemon juice

470ml/16fl oz iced water, with the ice cubes (about 3 parts cold water to 1 part ice)

1 egg yolk

115g/4oz flour, plus more for dredging

Vegetable, grapeseed or other neutral-flavoured oil

4 large or 8 small soft-shell crabs, cleaned

4 to 6 handfuls mesclun or other mixed salad greens

1 Place the butter in a small saucepan and turn the heat to medium-high. When the butter foam has subsided and the butter has browned lightly, add the passionfruit juice, salt and pepper to taste and lemon juice. Remove from the heat and keep warm.

2 Place the iced water in a bowl; add the egg yolk and beat for a moment. Add the flour and mix gently (Jean-Georges uses a chopstick for this); the batter should remain quite lumpy.

3 Add enough oil to a 30cm/12in frying pan to cover its bottom by 5mm/¼in. Turn the heat to high.

4 When the oil is hot (a pinch of flour will sizzle), dredge the crabs one at a time in the flour; shake off the excess, then drop them into the tempura batter. Transfer immediately to the hot oil. Cook on one side for 2 minutes, or until lightly browned, then turn over and cook on the other side until lightly browned. Drain on paper towels and salt them.

5 To serve, place the crabs on the greens and spoon the passionfruit sauce over all.

One day I arrived at Restaurant Jean-Georges to find the chef all in a lather. 'We have to do curried mussels,' he said. 'They are simply the best.' By that time, I had known Jean-Georges long enough to trust him; when he is excited about making a recipe, I am excited about eating it. 'Let's go,' I said.

We gathered ingredients, made curry powder and, 30 minutes after my arrival, sat down to one of the most delicious, if not bizarre, breakfasts of my life. I suggest you make this for dinner and soon. Eat with a spoon so you won't miss a drop of the sauce, and serve with Sticky Rice Steamed in Banana Leaves (page 145).

SERVES 4

CURRIED MUSSELS

2 tablespoons butter

2 shallots, minced

125ml/4fl oz fairly sweet white wine, such as a German Auslese

2kg/4lb mussels, trimmed of their beards and well washed

125ml/4fl oz crème fraîche or sour cream

1 teaspoon All-Purpose Curry Powder (page 214) or commercial curry powder, or to taste

1 tablespoon lemon juice

1 Place the butter in a saucepan large enough to contain the mussels and turn the heat to medium. When the butter melts, add the shallots and cook, stirring occasionally, for about 3 minutes until softened.

2 Add the white wine and the mussels, increase the heat to high and cover. Cook, shaking the pan occasionally, just until the mussels open, about 3 minutes.

3 Remove the mussels with a slotted spoon or strainer. Strain the liquid into a bowl, wipe out the pan, then return the liquid to the pan. Bring to the boil, then stir in the crème fraîche or sour cream and curry powder to taste.

4 Reduce the heat to medium-low and add the lemon juice; cook for about 3 minutes. Taste and adjust the seasoning as necessary, but don't add so much curry that it overpowers the other flavours. Return the mussels to the pot and stir to reheat. Serve, spooning the broth over the mussels.

This unique combination of flavours has been on the menu at Restaurant Jean-Georges since its opening and it continues to draw raves. The form of the layered scallops and cauliflower is basic but lovely, and the dark green sauce has a mysterious, mustardy flavour; few people could guess what is in it, and almost no one could imagine how simple it is.

Choose a rich starter, such as Mushroom Tarts with Onions and Walnuts (page 8), for a pleasant contrast.

SERVES 4

SCALLOPS AND CAULIFLOWER WITH CAPER-RAISIN SAUCE

50g/2oz capers, drained of all but 1 tablespoon of their liquid

50g/2oz golden raisins

8 to 12 cauliflower florets

50g/2oz butter

4 tablespoons vegetable, grapeseed or other neutral-flavoured oil

Salt and freshly ground black pepper

2 tablespoons minced parsley leaves

12 large sea scallops (at least 500g/1lb), cut in half through their equators

1/4 teaspoon freshly grated nutmeg, plus a little more

1 tablespoon sherry vinegar

1 Preheat the oven to 130°C/250°F/gas ½. Combine the capers and raisins in a small saucepan and add 160ml/6fl oz water; simmer gently until the raisins are plump, about 10 minutes. Do not cook rapidly; you don't want to reduce the liquid. Let the mixture cool for a couple of minutes, then purée it in a blender. Return it to the saucepan.

2 Meanwhile, use a sharp knife or mandoline to cut the cauliflower florets into 5mm/¼in-thick slices; you will need a total of 24 slices. Place 1 tablespoon each of butter and oil in a large frying pan and sauté the cauliflower over medium-high heat; do this in 2 or more batches to avoid crowding (add another tablespoon of butter or oil when necessary). Season it with salt and pepper as it cooks. Don't turn it too often; you want it to brown nicely. Total cooking time will be about 10 minutes, after which the cauliflower should be brown and crisp-tender. Remove and keep warm in a bowl in the oven.

3 Deglaze the pan by heating 4 tablespoons of water in it and stirring and scraping the bottom over high heat for a minute or two. Add the parsley and pour this juice over the cauliflower; gently stir and return the cauliflower to the oven while you cook the scallops.

4 Place 1 tablespoon each of butter and oil in another large ovenproof frying pan and turn the heat to medium-high. When the butter foams, add the scallops and cook on one side only until nicely browned, 2 to 3 minutes.

Again, do this in batches to avoid crowding (adding another tablespoon of butter or oil when necessary). Remove the scallops from the pan as they brown and season with salt and pepper; keep them warm in the oven.

5 Reheat the sauce, then add the nutmeg, vinegar and pepper and salt, if needed. Taste and adjust seasoning.

6 Spoon a little of the sauce onto each of 4 serving plates. Place 6 scallop pieces, browned side up, on each plate; top each scallop with a piece of cauliflower. Finish with a tiny grating of nutmeg.

If this dish sounds unusual, that's because it is. To develop it, Pierre Schutz – the chef at Vong in New York – began with a super-fragrant and eclectic spice mixture and continued with a standard French sauté of shellfish in butter.

Plain steamed asparagus goes with the sauce very nicely, or even a simple green salad will do. You may also substitute shrimps for the squid if you like, although the dish will not be as interesting.

SERVES 4

SCALLOPS AND SQUID WITH ASIAN SPICES, PAPRIKA AND BUTTER

2 cinnamon sticks

2 tablespoons allspice berries

2½ tablespoons coriander seeds

1 tablespoon All-Purpose Curry Powder (page 214) or commercial curry powder

2½ tablespoons turmeric

Pinch of saffron (optional)

Pinch of amchur (sour mango powder) (optional)

375g/¾lb squid, the bodies cleaned and cut into 1.2cm/½in rings, the tentacles washed and left whole

1 teaspoon hot paprika, preferably fresh and Hungarian

125ml/4fl oz semi-dry or sweet white wine

125ml/4fl oz Rich Chicken Stock (page 195) or other stock

90g/3oz butter

350g/¾lb scallops, cut in half through their equator if very large

Salt

1 tablespoon lemon juice

1 Toast the cinnamon sticks, allspice and coriander over medium-high heat in a dry frying pan until aromatic, for about 2 minutes. Combine with the curry powder, turmeric and saffron and amchur, if using, and grind finely in a spice or coffee grinder. (The mixture will keep in an opaque container at room temperature for at least a year.)

2 Toss the squid with the paprika.

3 Place the wine and stock in a small saucepan along with 2 teaspoons of the spice mix. Bring to the boil over high heat and cook, whisking frequently, until reduced to about 125ml/4fl oz, about 10 minutes. Reduce the heat to a minimum and start cooking the fish.

4 Place 2 tablespoons of butter in each of 2 frying pans, preferably nonstick, and turn the heat to high. When the butter foams, cook the scallops in one pan on one side only, for 2 to 3 minutes, until nicely browned. In the second frying pan, cook the squid undisturbed for 2 minutes, then toss and cook for another 30 seconds or so, until tender. Sprinkle both the scallops and squid with a little salt to taste when done.

5 While the shellfish is cooking, stir the remaining 2 tablespoons of butter into the sauce, along with salt to taste and the lemon juice. To serve, place a portion of the squid and scallops, browned sides face up, on each of 4 plates and spoon a little of the sauce over all.

On a foraging trip near my house, Jean-Georges and I collected bags of yarrow, which grows wild through-out much of the country. We used it to stuff shrimps. Later we played around with other herbs, and found dill and fennel to be the best. The lemon could be omitted from this recipe, but it's a nice technique that does more than warm and sweeten the fruit; try it.

Since this is a light dish, serve it with a hearty first course, such as Swiss Chard Timbales (page 12), Garlic Soup (page 26), or the glorious Asparagus Salad with Soy Vinaigrette and Hollandaise (page 40).

SERVES 4

DILL-STUFFED SHRIMPS WITH BAKED LEMON

2 lemons

3 heaping tablespoons sugar

24 large shrimps

3 tablespoons freshly snipped dill or fennel fronds

1 tablespoon minced garlic

2½ tablespoons extra virgin olive oil

Salt and cayenne pepper

1 Preheat the oven to 230°C/450°F/gas 8. Preheat the grill. (Alternatively, you can bake the lemons, then grill the shrimps in the same oven.)

2 Cut the pointed tips from the lemons, just enough so they'll sit flat. Cut the lemons in half, then place them, flesh sides up, in a baking tin; sprinkle with sugar. Bake for about 10 minutes, until the sugar melts and the pulp is soft.

3 Meanwhile, peel the shrimps; slice each one almost in half through their fronts to make a 'butterfly' shrimp that looks like this:)(. Mince the dill and sprinkle it over the insides of the shrimps. Close the shrimps.

4 Mix the garlic and oil. Brush on the shrimps, then sprinkle with salt and a pinch of cayenne.

5 Grill the shrimps, for 2 to 3 minutes per side, until done. Serve with the baked lemons, squeezing some of the lemon juice over the shrimps.

An East-West recipe that looks for all the world like shrimp marinara but tastes like nothing you've ever had before. You can substitute ginger, but it's worth a little effort to hunt down galangal, which has a sharper flavour. Be sure to mince the galangal very finely as it is somewhat woody otherwise.

Try a Pan-Fried Noodle Cake (page 144) with this.

SHRIMPS IN GALANGAL-TOMATO BROTH

4 tablespoons coriander seeds or ground coriander

1 clove

1 star anise

1½ tablespoons mace pieces or ground mace

½ tablespoon cardamom pods, crushed, seeds removed and pods discarded, or about ½ teaspoon cardamom seeds

½ teaspoon cayenne pepper, plus more to taste

5 tomatoes (about 1kg/2lb), cored and peeled

3 or 4 garlic cloves, peeled

1½ tablespoons plus 2 tablespoons extra virgin olive oil

50g/2oz butter

1 large onion, minced

1 tablespoon brown sugar

2 tablespoons peeled and very finely minced galangal (available at Asian markets) or ginger

1 Mix together the whole spices and toast, for about 2 minutes, over medium-high heat in a dry frying pan until aromatic. Combine with the ½ teaspoon cayenne and any powdered spices and grind finely in a spice or coffee grinder. (The mixture will keep in an opaque container, at room temperature, for at least a year.)

2 Cut the tomatoes in half through their equators; shake the seeds out into a bowl, then strain and reserve the juice.

3 Combine the garlic and 1½ tablespoons of olive oil in a small saucepan and cook together over medium heat, stirring occasionally, for about 10 minutes, until the garlic is golden brown.

4 Place the butter in a medium-to-large frying pan and turn the heat to medium-high. When the foam subsides, add the onion and, when it begins to soften – about 3 minutes later – add the brown sugar, galangal, lemon zest, sautéed garlic and its oil, and 2 tablespoons of the spice mixture. Season lightly with salt.

5 Cook for 2 minutes, then add the rice vinegar. Increase the heat to high and cook, stirring and scraping the bottom of the pan, for about a minute. Add the tomatoes, then the strained tomato juice and 470ml/8fl oz water. Add the mango and basil and reduce the heat to medium-low; cook for about 45 minutes at a low simmer.

6 Strain the sauce and place the tomato 'jam' in one saucepan and the liquid in another. Season each with salt and pepper to taste, a teaspoon or

Zest of 1 lemon, minced

Salt

2 tablespoons rice vinegar

1/2 mango, peeled and diced

10 basil leaves

Freshly ground black pepper

2 teaspoons lemon juice, or a little more to taste

750g–1kg/1½–2lb medium-to-large shrimps, peeled

1 teaspoon fresh thyme leaves or ½ teaspoon dried thyme

more of lemon juice and a little cayenne; taste and adjust seasoning as necessary and keep warm.

7 Sprinkle the shrimps with salt, cayenne and thyme. Place the remaining 2 tablespoons of olive oil in a large frying pan over high heat; a minute later add the shrimps. Cook until pink and opaque, turning once, for a total of 3 or 4 minutes.

8 To serve, shape a small pile of the tomato jam in the centre of each of 4 or 6 bowls with a small ice cream scoop or two spoons. Spoon the tomato liquid around it and arrange the shrimps in the liquid. Serve hot.

There is a lot to do here, and many ingredients to gather, but the result is a lobster dish with a lovely, rust-brown sauce and a deep, mysterious flavour that will keep everyone guessing. None of the techniques is difficult and you can prepare everything in advance, waiting until the last minute to sauté the lobster meat, toast the bread and give the broth its final seasoning.

A simple salad will complement this; try Beetroot and Ginger Salad (page 42) or Mushroom Salad with Cider Vinegar and Coriander (page 49).

SERVES 4

LOBSTER WITH PUMPKIN SEED BROTH

2 stalks lemongrass

2 large tomatoes (about 500g/1lb), roughly chopped

1 tablespoon honey

1 tablespoon soy sauce

4 lobsters, each about 625–750g/1¼–1½lb

1 tablespoon vegetable, grapeseed or other neutral-flavoured oil

1 medium onion, roughly chopped

1 celery stalk, roughly chopped

1 carrot, roughly chopped

1 tablespoon tomato purée

375ml/13fl oz dry white wine

375ml/13fl oz Rich Chicken Stock (page 195), Dark Chicken Stock (page 196), or other stock

2½ tablespoons toasted hulled pumpkin seeds

1 Trim the lemongrass of its tough outer leaves and thinly slice it. Combine with the tomatoes, honey and soy sauce. Set aside.

2 Blanch the lobsters by plunging them into rapidly boiling water to cover for 1 minute. Remove and plunge them into iced water. Break off the tails and claws. Remove the meat from the claws and cut the tails, still in the shell, in half crosswise; set them aside. Break off the heads and discard. Roughly chop the small legs and the bodies.

3 Place the oil in a large, deep frying pan or saucepan and turn the heat to medium-high. Toss in the lobster bodies, along with the onion, celery and carrot. Cook for 2 minutes, stirring occasionally, then add the tomato purée. Stir in the wine and stock 5 minutes later; bring to the boil, then reduce the heat and simmer for 30 minutes.

4 Meanwhile, mix together the pumpkin seeds, almonds, coriander, fenugreek, sesame and cardamom in a dry frying pan; toast over medium heat, shaking almost constantly, for 3 to 5 minutes, until aromatic. Use a spice or coffee grinder to grind to a powder.

5 Strain the stock-lobster mixture, pressing to extract as much liquid as possible; there will be about 470ml/16fl oz. Place it in a clean saucepan along with the tomato-lemongrass mixture and 125ml/4fl oz of the spice mixture.

SIMPLE GOOD FOOD

2 tablespoons slivered almonds, blanched

1 tablespoon coriander seeds

1 tablespoon fenugreek seeds

2 tablespoons sesame seeds

2 cardamom pods, crushed, seeds removed, pods discarded

1 bunch fresh mint, stems and all

4 thick slices sourdough rye or other good bread

40g/1½oz butter

Salt and freshly ground black pepper

1 tablespoon lime or lemon juice

16 snow peas, trimmed

6 Bring to the boil and simmer for 10 minutes, then toss in the mint. Turn off the heat, cover, and let rest while you prepare the remaining ingredients. (You may prepare the recipe in advance up to this point; refrigerate the lobster meat and broth separately, well-wrapped or in covered containers, for up to 1 day.)

7 Use the grill or a toaster to toast the bread; place 1 piece each in shallow soup bowls.

8 Place ⅔ of the butter in a frying pan and turn the heat to medium-high. When the foam subsides, add the lobster tails and cook, stirring, for 2 minutes. Add the claw meat and cook for another minute or two, until everything is nicely browned and firm. Sprinkle lightly with salt and pepper.

9 Strain the broth, reheat it and stir in the lime or lemon juice and remaining 1 tablespoon of butter. Taste and add salt and pepper as necessary.

10 Blanch the snow peas in boiling salted water to cover for 1 minute; drain.

11 To assemble, arrange the cooked lobster on the bread and scatter the snow peas around it. Pour the steaming hot broth around everything and serve immediately.

To create this dish, Jean-Georges took a classic French *nage* (cooking shrimps and lobster in an aromatic broth) and added Asian seasonings – but, for added complexity, he left some of the French ones in. Although there are a lot of ingredients here, the assembly is easy and the results are well worth the effort. If you want to use lobster meat, buy two lobsters, each about 750g/1½lb, and blanch them according to the directions in Lobster with Pumpkin Seed Broth (page 66).

You don't need a side dish with this, but you might begin the meal with the Leek Terrine (page 6) or the Mushroom Tarts with Onions and Walnuts (page 8).

SERVES 4

SHRIMPS OR LOBSTER IN SPICY BROTH

25g/1oz butter

1 leek, white part only, split, well washed and roughly chopped

1 medium carrot, roughly chopped

1 shallot, roughly chopped

1 celery stalk, roughly chopped

Salt

¼ teaspoon cumin seeds

¼ teaspoon fenugreek seeds or ground fenugreek

1 tablespoon coriander seeds, lightly crushed in a pestle and mortar or with the bottom of a pot

1 thyme sprig

Zest of 1 orange, white insides scraped off

Pinch of cayenne pepper

1 Place half the butter in a frying pan or large saucepan and turn the heat to high. Add the leek, carrot, shallot and celery and a sprinkling of salt, along with the cumin, fenugreek, coriander, thyme, orange zest and cayenne.

2 Cook, stirring, for 1 minute, then add the wine, stock and 250ml/8fl oz of water. Remove the stems from the mushrooms and throw them in as well.

3 Bring to the boil, reduce the heat to medium, and simmer for 30 minutes; the mixture should be bubbling, but not boiling rapidly.

4 Cut the mushroom caps in half if they're small, in thick slices if they're large.

5 You can eat the vegetables used to make the broth, but if you want a better presentation, prepare the 3 optional vegetables listed. Trim them and, if they are large, cut them into bite-sized pieces. Blanch in boiling water to cover for 3 or 4 minutes, just until tender, and set aside.

6 In another saucepan, combine the mushroom caps, shrimps or lobster, and the optional blanched vegetables, or the strained vegetables from the broth (remove the thyme, orange zest and any whole spices). Strain the broth over

125ml/4fl oz semi-dry or sweet wine

125ml/4fl oz Rich Chicken Stock
(page 195), Dark Chicken Stock
(page 196), or other stock or water

125g/4oz button mushrooms

125g/4oz spring onions or baby
onions (optional)

125g/4oz baby or larger turnips
(optional)

125g/4oz baby or larger carrots
(optional)

750g/1½lb medium-to-large
shrimps, peeled, or lightly cooked
lobster meat, cut into chunks

1 tablespoon lemon juice

1 tablespoon fresh tarragon, roughly
chopped

2 tablespoons fresh chervil, roughly
chopped

2 tablespoons parsley leaves,
roughly chopped

Coarse sea salt

this, and add the remaining butter. Increase the heat to high and cook until the shrimps are pink and opaque or the lobster heated through, just about 4 minutes. Remove the shrimps and vegetables and place them in 4 bowls.

7 Return the broth to the heat and taste; add salt and cayenne if necessary, together with the lemon juice. Stir in the fresh herbs and spoon the broth over the shrimps or lobster. Finish with a sprinkling of coarse sea salt and serve.

This seafood cassoulet – which was inspired by Louis Outhier, Jean-Georges's most important mentor – is ideal in late summer, when fresh shell beans are in season. But it's also wonderful with dried beans – pinto, cranberry (borlotti), or pink – in the middle of winter.

Serve it with a light salad, such as Beetroot and Ginger (page 42) or Fennel and Apple with Juniper (page 48).

SERVES 4

BORLOTTI BEANS WITH SEAFOOD

250g/½lb shelled fresh borlotti beans or 200g/7oz dried borlotti, pinto, or pink beans

Top 8cm/3in of a celery stalk, with leaves

1 bay leaf

1 thyme sprig or ¼ teaspoon dried thyme

1 medium leek, trimmed, split in half, well washed and roughly chopped

Salt

4 tablespoons extra virgin olive oil

15 medium-to-large shrimps, peeled

24 clams (the smaller the better), well scrubbed

125ml/4fl oz dry white wine

500g/1lb squid, cleaned, the bodies cut into rings

Freshly ground black pepper

25g/1oz butter

2 tablespoons sherry vinegar

4 to 6 handfuls salad greens

Minced parsley

1 Place the beans, celery, bay leaf, thyme and leek in a saucepan with water to cover. Turn the heat to medium-high and cook, stirring and tasting occasionally, for 15 to 20 minutes for fresh beans, 45 to 90 minutes for dried beans, until tender. Drain and salt them when they're done and keep warm.

2 Place 1 tablespoon of olive oil in a large ovenproof frying pan and turn the heat to medium high. Add the shrimps and cook on both sides until pink, for a total of about 4 minutes. Place the frying pan in a low oven to keep warm.

3 Place 1½ tablespoons of olive oil in a saucepan or deep frying pan and turn the heat to high. Almost immediately, add the clams and the white wine. Cover, reduce the heat to medium and cook, shaking the pan frequently. When the first clams begin to open – it could take as little as 3 minutes or as long as 10 – add the squid and replace the lid. Cook, shaking, until all the clams are open and the squid is opaque, just a few more minutes.

4 Remove the clams and squid with a slotted spoon; when the clams are cool enough to handle, take the meat from the shells (leave a few clams intact, as a garnish). Return the clams and squid to their cooking liquid and turn the heat to low. Add the remaining 1½ tablespoons of olive oil, pepper to taste (and salt, if necessary, but remember that the clam liquid is very salty), the butter and the sherry vinegar. Stir in the beans.

5 Divide the greens onto each of 4 plates. Top with a portion of beans and seafood, and garnish with 4 shrimps and a reserved whole clam or two. Garnish with parsley and serve.

A simple, clean broth that is nicely complemented by bay-scented cod. The technique of tucking bay leaves under the skin is frequently used with chicken but rarely seen with fish; it's an easy but sophisticated touch. This dish is even better with a few hardshell (littleneck or cherrystone) clams added to the simmering broth. It's also nice with a side dish of Beetroot Tartare (page 43).

SERVES 4

SAUTÉED COD WITH BAY LEAVES AND POTATOES

Four 175–225g/6–8oz cod fillets, skin on (or 1 or 2 larger pieces)

9 bay leaves

2 large potatoes (about 500g/1lb), peeled and cut into 5mm/¼in dice

3 tablespoons extra virgin olive oil

1 medium onion, thinly sliced

3 thyme sprigs or ½ teaspoon dried thyme

470ml/16fl oz Dark Chicken Stock (page 195), Rich Chicken Stock (page 196), or other stock

Salt and freshly ground black pepper

Coarse sea salt

1 Preheat the oven to 250°C/475°F/gas 9. Use a thin-bladed knife to peel back the skin of the cod, leaving the skin attached at one end. Tuck 2 bay leaves under the skin of each piece, then pat the skin back into place. Set aside while you prepare the broth.

2 Rinse the potatoes in cold water to remove excess starch. Heat 1½ table-spoons of olive oil in a large, deep frying pan or broad saucepan and add the potatoes, onion, thyme and remaining bay leaf. Cook for 1 minute, stirring, then add the stock. Bring to the boil and keep the heat medium-high so the mixture bubbles, but not furiously. Season with salt and pepper. When the potatoes are tender and the liquid reduced by about half – this will take 10 to 15 minutes – reduce the heat to low.

3 When the broth is nearly done, add the remaining oil to a large ovenproof frying pan and turn the heat to high. A minute later add the cod, skin side down. Cook for 1 minute, then transfer to the oven.

4 Roast for about 8 minutes, until the cod is opaque and tender throughout – a thin-bladed knife inserted into its centre will meet little resistance. Ladle some potatoes and a little liquid into each of 4 bowls, then top with a piece of fish. Sprinkle all with salt and serve.

A light potato and clam 'chowder' (cream), with a light, bright parsley purée. The sauce will complement any white fish you like, from tender cod to firmer red snapper or monkfish, or anything in between. Just make sure the fish is skinned and filleted.

This is one of the few dishes in this book that is best served with crusty bread. If you'd like a first course, try the Swiss Chard Timbales (page 12) or Quiche of Chicken Livers and Mushrooms (page 13).

SERVES 4

COD WITH CLAMS AND PARSLEY SAUCE

250ml/8fl oz dry white wine

1 tablespoon butter

1 shallot, minced

1 garlic clove, minced

24 clams, each about 4–5cm/1½–2in in diameter, rinsed

125g/4oz parsley leaves (some very thin stems are okay), loosely packed

6 tablespoons vegetable, grapeseed or other neutral-flavoured oil

Salt

4 spring onions, slivered the long way, or 25g/1oz chives, cut into 2.5cm/1in pieces

½ teaspoon freshly ground black pepper

4 fillets of skinless cod or other fish, each about 175g/6oz, or 1 or 2 larger pieces

¼ teaspoon cayenne pepper

Olive oil or butter as needed

1 Combine the wine, butter, shallot and garlic in a large saucepan over high heat. When the mixture boils, add the clams. Cover and cook, shaking the pan occasionally, until the clams open, about 10 minutes. Cool slightly, then strain the liquid and reserve 470ml/16fl oz (discard the rest). Preheat the oven to 250°C/475°F/gas 9.

2 While the clams are cooking, wash the parsley well and leave it wet. Place the parsley, oil and ½ teaspoon salt in a blender. Add 2 tablespoons of water and purée, adding a little more water if necessary to enable the machine to work. When the mixture is smooth, set aside.

3 Remove the clams from their shells and chop them into 3 or 4 pieces each. Place them in a small saucepan with the reserved clam broth, spring onions or chives, and the black pepper. Turn the heat to medium.

4 Heat a large non-stick ovenproof frying pan over high heat; sprinkle the pieces of fish with some salt and cayenne. Film the bottom of the frying pan with a little olive oil or butter; pour out the excess. Add the fish and cook for 1 minute, then transfer the pan to the oven.

5 Stir the parsley purée into the simmering broth and keep warm. Flip the fish after 3 or 4 minutes, when it is brown on the first side. Roast for another 2 to 4 minutes, until it is cooked through (a thin-bladed knife inserted into its middle will meet little resistance).

6 Place a piece of fish in each of 4 bowls, then spoon in a portion of the broth, with the clams and spring onions or chives. Serve immediately.

Here's a recipe you can make with whatever vegetables you have on hand, since the defining ingredients are fresh fish and fresh herbs. It's made into a saucy dish by adding a little water during the final stage of cooking.

Although this is a perfect one-pot meal, it wouldn't hurt to begin with a bowl of Creamy Butternut Squash Soup (page 29).

SERVES 4

HALIBUT STEAKS WITH MIXED VEGETABLES

Two 300–350g/10–12oz halibut steaks

Salt and cayenne pepper

Flour for dredging

2 tablespoons extra virgin olive oil

15g/½oz butter

2 garlic cloves, lightly crushed

4 thyme sprigs

12 medium asparagus stalks, peeled

1 medium courgette, cut into eight 5-mm/¼-in-thick slices

8 artichoke hearts, preferably fresh but frozen are fine

1 large tomato, peeled, seeds and pulp discarded, flesh cut into rough chunks (not small dice)

2 tablespoons pitted black salt-cured olives

75g/2½oz fresh or frozen and thawed peas

Freshly ground black pepper

2 tablespoons roughly chopped basil

Coarse sea salt

1 Sprinkle the fish with salt and cayenne, then dredge lightly in the flour, shaking off the excess. Place a large, heavy saucepan or frying pan, preferably nonstick, over high heat. A minute later, add the olive oil and butter. When the butter melts, place the halibut in the pan, with the garlic and thyme around it.

2 Cook for 1 minute, then add the asparagus, courgette and artichokes. Reduce the heat to medium-high and cover the pan. About 4 minutes later, when the underside of the halibut is browned, turn it. Add 125ml/4fl oz of water, together with the tomato and olives. Replace the lid and cook for 2 more minutes.

3 Remove the halibut, which should be slightly underdone, and keep it warm in a 100°C/200°F/gas ¼ oven. Replace the lid and continue to cook the vegetables for another 2 minutes, adding a little water if necessary. The mixture should be loose, but not at all soupy. Add the peas and increase the heat to high. Season the vegetable mixture with salt and pepper, then return the fish to the pan. Cook for another minute or two, scooping the vegetables and the juice onto the fish.

4 Cover and turn off the heat; leave the dish to rest for a minute. Remove the fish and vegetables to plates, then garnish with the basil and a little coarse salt. Eat with a spoon.

A magnificent, yet simple, presentation of classic papillote – food wrapped in parchment paper, which when heated swells and puffs up. Here the papillote is cooked on top of the stove instead of in the oven, in an aluminum foil package that blows up like a balloon. The super-moist and flavourful fish really belies the ease of preparation. The packages take little time to assemble but can be stored, wrapped and refrigerated, for up to 3 hours before cooking. And the result itself is dramatic and fun.

To serve four people, make two separate packages and cook them at the same time. Or, use this amount for four first course helpings. Serve with Corn Cake (page 142), Millet Cake (page 143), or Pan-Fried Noodle Cake (page 144).

SERVES 2

HALIBUT EN PAPILLOTE

¼ small white or savoy cabbage (about 125g/4oz), cored and separated into leaves, then shredded

Two 175g/6oz fillets of halibut, salmon, cod, red snapper, etc., about 2.5cm/1in thick

Freshly ground black pepper

50g/2oz shiitake mushrooms, stems removed and discarded or saved for stock, caps roughly chopped

1 large tomato (about 250g/½lb), peeled, deseeded and roughly chopped

Butter for the foil, plus 2 tablespoons

12–15 whole mint leaves

4–6 sprigs whole coriander leaves

2 tablespoons nam pla or nuoc mam (Asian fish sauce)

2 tablespoons lime juice

1 tablespoon any oil

Coarse sea salt

1 Blanch the cabbage in boiling salted water to cover for about 2 minutes, until just tender. Rinse under cold water to stop the cooking, then drain.

2 Make a stack of 3 pieces of 1-m/3-ft-long sheets of aluminium foil. Have the short end facing you and butter it halfway up to the other end. On the butterred foil, place the cabbage, fish, pepper, mushrooms and tomato. Cut the 2 tablespoons of butter into bits and dot the pile with it. Then scatter the mint, coriander, nam pla and lime juice over the pile.

3 Fold one short end onto the other, then fold the foil onto itself the long way. Crimp the edges as tightly as possible by making 3–5cm/1–2in folds, one after the other, each sealing the other. The package must be very tightly sealed, but leave plenty of room around the fish.

4 Place a frying pan large enough to fit the package over high heat. A minute later, add the oil, then pour out all but a film. Put the package directly into the pan, it will sizzle. About 2 minutes later, the package will expand like a balloon; be careful of escaping steam. Cook for 5 to 6 minutes from that point (less for salmon, more for halibut).

5 Remove the package from the heat, still taking care to avoid any escaping steam. Leave to rest for 1 minute, then cut a slit along the length of the top with a knife. Use a knife and fork to open up the package, then spoon the fish and vegetables onto a plate. Top with salt and serve.

Jean-Georges first learned a recipe for white fish in a sweet wine sauce from Louis Outhier, his most important teacher. He's refined it over the years and made it drier and simpler. The flavour here will surprise you, especially considering the simplicity of the ingredients. You can substitute chicken stock for the 'Jacqueline,' but at the cost of some complexity in the final dish.

You don't really need a side dish here (crusty bread is nice), but you might start with an unusual salad, such as Endive and Black Olive (page 47) or Beetroot and Ginger (page 42).

SERVES 4

HALIBUT IN SHERRY SAUCE

470ml/16fl oz 'Jacqueline' Broth (page 199)

750g/1½lb halibut fillet (the 4 sections cut out of each steak)

125g/4oz butter

Salt and freshly ground black pepper

2½ tablespoons dry (fino) sherry

2 tomatoes, cored, peeled, seeded, and cut into 5mm/¼in dice

2 small courgettes, cut into 5mm/¼in dice

Cayenne pepper

1 Place the 'Jacqueline' broth in a small saucepan and turn the heat to high; reduce the broth until it is quite syrupy, about 125ml/4fl oz in volume; this will take at least 15 minutes from the time it begins to boil.

2 Meanwhile, 'butterfly' the halibut fillets by cutting them almost in half through their equators, then flattening them out with your hand. Preheat the oven to 250°C/475°F/gas 9.

3 When the Jacqueline is ready, reduce the heat and stir in a quarter of the butter, along with salt and pepper to taste. When the butter melts, add the sherry, stir, and remove from the heat.

4 Place half the remaining butter in a 25cm/10in frying pan, turn the heat to high and add the tomatoes and courgettes. Cook for just 2 or 3 minutes, until the tomatoes become a little juicy and the courgettes bright green and glossy (and remain slightly crisp).

5 At more or less the same time, place the rest of the butter in a 25–30-cm/10–12-in ovenproof frying pan and turn the heat to medium-high. When the butter is barely melted, add the fish and sprinkle it with salt and cayenne. After 2 minutes, flip the fish and put the pan in the oven for 3 minutes, or until the fish is barely cooked through.

6 When the halibut goes into the oven, reheat the sauce quickly and spoon a puddle of it onto each of 4 plates. Reheat the vegetables, if necessary. Place a piece of fish on top of the sauce, then spoon some vegetables onto it. Drizzle with any remaining sauce and serve.

With or without the Green Tomato Marmalade (page 136), this spicy dish must be served with a spoon; the broth is good enough to drink. If you do not have any Fish Fumet (page 198), you have two options:

Use Rich Chicken Stock (page 195), which will give you a different, but still good, set of flavours; or make the fumet on the spot, with bones bought at the same time as the fillets – any fishmonger will give you some.

 # POACHED FISH WITH FENNEL

2 tablespoons fennel seeds

6 peppercorns

6 coriander seeds

2 lemons

40g/1½oz butter

4 spring onions, trimmed and minced

2 bay leaves

Four 175g/6oz fillets (or use 2 larger fillets) of red snapper, sea bass or other firm-fleshed white fish, skinned

Salt and cayenne pepper

900ml/1½ pints Fish Fumet (page 198)

2 tablespoons lemon juice

Minced fennel fronds or chervil for garnish

Green Tomato Marmalade (page 136) optional

1 Preheat the oven to 250°C/475°F/gas 9. Crush the fennel seeds, peppercorns and coriander seeds together with the side of a knife, then mince, but not to a powder.

2 Peel the zests from the lemons and place the zests in a small saucepan with water to cover. Bring to the boil; then drain, rinse and dry. Section the lemons as you would a grapefruit; set the sections aside.

3 Spread a little of the butter over the bottom of a flameproof baking dish. Place the spring onions and bay leaves in it. Sprinkle each side of the fillets with salt, cayenne, and about ½ teaspoon of the spice mix. Place the fillets on top of the spring onions and scatter the blanched lemon zest around them. Pour the Fish Fumet into the dish.

4 Bring the mixture to the boil on top of the stove, then place the baking dish in the oven. Turn over the fillets after 3 minutes, then remove the dish 2 minutes later. Remove the fillets and place them on a warm platter; put the baking dish back on the stove over high heat.

5 Stir in the remaining butter, along with some cayenne and salt, if necessary. Add the lemon juice and stir.

6 Serve the fish in bowls, with the broth all around it. Garnish with the bay leaves, the reserved lemon sections and the fennel or chervil. Add a small scoop of Green Tomato Marmalade to the bowls if you like.

You need fish bones and a variety of spices for this nutty, North African-style fish stew, which was developed by Vong chef Pierre Schutz, but the procedure is quick and easy. Serve with peeled asparagus spears and trimmed spring onions, cooked together in boiling water for about 5 minutes.

It's great with Sticky Rice Steamed in Banana Leaves (page 145), or on its own. You might precede it with something simple, such as Tomato Towers with Basil (page 2).

SERVES 4

MONKFISH WITH ALMONDS AND SPICES

2 tablespoons shelled almonds

2 tablespoons coriander seeds

2 tablespoons sesame seeds

2 tablespoons hazelnuts

2 tablespoons sumac berries (optional)

2 tablespoons cumin seeds

90g/3oz butter

500g/1lb meaty bones from any white-fleshed fish

Zest of 1 orange, blanched in boiling water for a minute and drained

Zest of 1 lemon, blanched in boiling water for a minute and drained

2 tablespoons ground turmeric

470ml/16fl oz Rich Chicken Stock (page 195) or other chicken stock

1kg/2lb monkfish, preferably on the bone (a little less if it has been boned)

1 tablespoon lime juice

Salt

Minced coriander

1 Combine the almonds, coriander, sesame, hazelnuts, sumac berries, if using, and cumin in a dry frying pan and toast over medium heat, shaking the pan occasionally, until nice and fragrant, for 2 to 3 minutes. Cool slightly, then grind coarsely in a spice grinder.

2 Melt ⅓ of the butter over medium-high heat in a large frying pan; add the fish bones and cook, stirring, for about 5 minutes. Add the citrus zest, 50g/2oz of the spice mixture and the turmeric. Stir and cook for 1 minute.

3 Add the stock and 250ml/9fl oz of water and bring to the boil. Reduce the heat to medium low and simmer for 30 minutes. Strain, pressing on the fish bones to extract as much liquid as possible.

4 Melt ⅓ of the butter in a large frying pan over medium-high heat. Sear the monkfish lightly on both sides, for a total of about 3 minutes. Add the fish broth and continue to cook, now over medium heat, turning the fish frequently.

5 When there is about 250ml/9fl oz of liquid remaining and the fish is tender – about 10 minutes later – add the remaining butter, together with the lime juice and salt to taste. Remove the fish to serving plates and spoon on some sauce. Garnish with coriander and a few more pinches of the spice mixture and serve immediately.

This is a simply brilliant technique you'll want to use all the time – it works beautifully with salmon here, and with other fish (such as halibut or cod) as well, giving you moist, nicely cooked results. In the restaurants' convection ovens, Jean-Georges cooks the fish at 100°/200°/gas 1/2, but a home oven must be set to 140°/275°F/gas 1 to get the same results.

Beetroot Tartare (page 43) goes well as a side dish here, or you might begin with Garlic Soup (page 26), Parsley Soup with Mixed Mushrooms (page 28), or Fresh Pea Soup (page 30).

SERVES 4

GENTLY COOKED SALMON WITH MASHED POTATOES

1kg/2lb baking potatoes (about 5 or 6), peeled and cut into quarters

50g/2oz butter

One 750g/1½lb centre-cut salmon fillet (or two 375g/¾lb fillets), about 3cm/1¼in thick at thickest point, skin on and scaled

15g/½oz chives (about 40 to 60 chives or a small handful)

3 tablespoons vegetable, grapeseed or other neutral-flavoured oil

Salt

175ml/6oz milk, gently warmed

Freshly ground black pepper

Coarse sea salt and cracked black pepper

1 Boil the potatoes in salted water to cover, until soft; this will take about 20–30 minutes.

2 Meanwhile, smear a baking tin with ¼ teaspoon of the butter and place the salmon, skin side up, on the butter. Leave to sit while you preheat the oven to 140°C/275°F/gas 1.

3 Mince a tablespoon or so of the chives for garnishing. Tear the rest of the chives into 5cm/2in lengths and place in a blender with the oil and a little salt. Blend, stopping the machine to scrape down the mixture once or twice, until the oil has a creamlike consistency.

4 When the potatoes are soft, put the salmon in the oven and set the timer for 12 minutes.

5 Drain the potatoes, then mash them well or put through a food mill. Return them to the pot over very low heat and stir in the remaining butter and – gradually – the milk, beating with a wooden spoon until smooth and creamy. Season with salt and pepper as necessary. Keep warm.

6 Check the salmon after 12 minutes; the skin should peel off easily, it should flake, and an instant-read thermometer should read about 50°C/120°F. The fish may look underdone, but if it meets these three criteria it is done. (If it is not done, or if you prefer it better done, return it to the oven for 3 minutes more.) If you like, scrape off the grey fatty matter on the skin side (or just turn the fish over). Sprinkle with some salt and pepper.

7 To serve, place a portion of mashed potatoes on a plate; top with a piece of salmon. Drizzle chive oil all around the plate and garnish with minced chives.

Another use for Jean-Georges's 'Jacqueline' Broth, but in this recipe it's scented with cardamom, which is the catalyst for an exotic transformation.

This meal-in-a-pot needs no side dish, but if you'd like a starter, choose Rice Paper Rolls of Shrimps and Herbs (page 14), Shrimp Satay (page 17), or a simple salad, such as Fennel and Apple Salad with Juniper (page 48).

SERVES 4

SALMON IN CARDAMOM BROTH

900ml/1½ pints 'Jacqueline' Broth (page 199)

1 scant tablespoon cardamom pods or 1 teaspoon ground cardamom

125g/4oz peeled baby turnips or 2 medium turnips, peeled and cut into 2.5-cm/1-in chunks

4 handfuls arugula, washed, dried, and roughly chopped if the leaves are large

Four 175g/6oz salmon fillets

Salt and cayenne pepper

2 tablespoons extra virgin olive oil

40g/1½oz butter

2 medium ripe tomatoes, peeled, deseeded and cut into 2.5-cm/1-in dice

1 Bring the 'Jacqueline' broth to a fast boil and reduce by about one-quarter, so that there are about 750ml/1¼ pints of liquid. Add the cardamom and leave over low heat for 10 minutes. Strain out the pods if you used them.

2 Meanwhile, blanch the turnips in boiling salted water until tender; plunge them into iced water to stop the cooking, drain and set aside. Preheat the oven to 250°C/475°F/gas 9.

3 Return the stock to the pot over medium-low heat. Divide the arugula among 4 bowls. Season the salmon with salt and cayenne.

4 Place an ovenproof frying pan over high heat for 2 or 3 minutes. Add the oil, then the salmon, skin side down. Cook for 1 minute, then place in the oven. Roast for about 5 minutes, a little longer if the pieces are thick or you like your salmon well done.

5 While the salmon roasts, season the broth with salt and cayenne. Add the butter; when it melts, add the turnips and tomatoes.

6 Place the salmon on the arugula, skin side up. Spoon the vegetables and broth around the arugula, not over the salmon; serve immediately.

The sole challenge to preparing this attractively layered dish lies in taking the time to make the twelve flat lacy potato crisps; that time can be cut in half by using two frying pans, but you'll still need to spend 30 minutes at the stove. The other aspects of this creation are simple: baked salmon and a quick sauce made from lightly whipped cream mixed with celery and horseradish.

When buying salmon for this dish, ask for a middle-cut slice of uniform thickness; you will be cutting it into twelve 2-cm/½-in-thick scallops.

Start with something simple, such as the Creamy Butternut Squash Soup (page 29) or the Fresh Pea Soup (page 30).

SERVES 4

SALMON AND POTATO CRISPS

2 large baking potatoes, just over 500g/1lb

1 small or ½ large celeriac, peeled

About 125ml/4fl oz extra virgin olive oil

Salt

1 celery stalk

1 small piece fresh horseradish root, or 2 tablespoons prepared horseradish

150ml/5fl oz double cream

Cayenne pepper

135ml/4½fl oz lemon juice

A bunch of minced chives

750g/1½lb middle-cut salmon fillet

1 Peel the potatoes but do not wash them; their starch enables them to stick together. Trim the celeriac of all brown spots; set a small piece of it aside. Use the julienne blade of a mandoline or food processor to make a fine julienne of both the potatoes and celeriac, and mix them together.

2 Place about 1 tablespoon of olive oil in a 25cm/10in nonstick frying pan and turn the heat to medium-high. When it is hot (a piece of the potato mixture will sizzle), scatter about 25g/1oz of the potato–celeriac mixture loosely over the surface of the oil; the object is to make a lacy doily of the mixture. It's not difficult; the key is to not put too much of the mixture in the pan; you can always add a few more strands. Just make certain you do not completely cover the bottom of the pan. Cook, encouraging the outer strands to stick to those in the middle by prodding with a spatula, until lightly browned on one side; do not let the pancake become too crisp. Turn and cook the other side, then drain on paper towels and sprinkle with salt. Repeat, adding more oil as necessary (they don't absorb much, so don't overdo it). It's easiest to have two pans going at once, and feel free to make these several hours in advance; just reheat the crisps in the oven as you cook the salmon.

3 Using the finest grater you have, grate enough of the reserved small piece of celeriac to make 1 tablespoon. Grate enough of the celery to make

1 tablespoon. Grate enough of the horseradish to make 1 tablespoon. Set aside for a moment.

4   Lightly beat the cream; it should be soft and thick, but not hold even a soft peak. Stir in the grated vegetables, then season with cayenne and salt to taste. Stir in 2 teaspoons of the lemon juice and 2 tablespoons of the chives.

5   Use a carving or slicing knife to cut the salmon on a 20° to 30° angle into twelve 2-cm/½-in-thick slices. Place them in a shallow roasting pan and sprinkle them with salt, cayenne and 4 tablespoons each of the remaining olive oil and lemon juice. Leave to sit while you preheat the oven to 200°C/400°F/gas 6; turn over once after about 5 minutes.

6   Place the salmon and its marinade in the oven. Roast for about 2 minutes, then turn over; roast for another 2 minutes or so, until the salmon is pale on the outside but still a little rosy within.

7   Place a piece of salmon on each of 4 plates, then cover it with a potato pancake. Repeat, making 3 layers on each plate. Garnish with minced chives and serve with the celery-horseradish cream.

The Provençal-style combination of potatoes, tomatoes and tapenade is sheer delight, and perhaps the most difficult aspect is to avoid eating the Tomato Confit (page 135) as soon as you make it. The self-denial is worth it, however.

SERVES 4

No side dish is necessary. For a starter, consider Tomato Towers with Basil (page 2), Leek Terrine (page 6) or Garlic Soup (page 26).

RED SNAPPER WITH TOMATO CONFIT AND TAPENADE

About 375g/¾lb new potatoes

Several sprigs thyme, tarragon or sage

2 garlic cloves

Salt

250g/½lb pitted black olives

2 anchovy fillets

About 250ml/9fl oz extra virgin olive oil

About 5 large basil leaves

1 teaspoon sherry vinegar

2 small courgettes (about 250g/½lb), trimmed

Freshly ground black pepper

2 large red snapper, striped bass, or sea bass fillets, skin on (about 625–750g/1¼–1½lb total)

Cayenne pepper

12 tomatoes from Tomato Confit (page 135), with their olive oil, placed on a baking tray

1 Put the potatoes in a small saucepan with water to cover; add the herbs, garlic and a hefty pinch of salt. Cook until just tender but not at all mushy, 20 to 30 minutes. Cool, peel, then cut into 5-mm/¼-in-thick slices and set aside. Preheat the oven to 250°C/475°F/gas 9.

2 To make the tapenade, combine the olives, anchovies, 125ml/4fl oz of olive oil, basil and sherry vinegar in a blender. Whir until smooth, stopping the machine and scraping down as necessary. Place in a small serving bowl.

3 Cut the courgettes into long strips about 3mm/⅛in thick (use a mandoline if you have one).

4 Heat 3 frying pans (your life will be easier if they're nonstick and one should be ovenproof) over medium heat. In the first, place 2 tablespoons of olive oil and turn the heat to medium-high. Add the potato slices, season them with salt and pepper and cook, turning over only once or twice after each side browns.

5 While the potatoes cook, add 1 tablespoon of olive oil and 2 tablespoons of water to the second pan. Add the courgettes and cook over medium-high heat, tossing occasionally, for about 5 minutes, or until tender but not mushy.

6 Meanwhile, add 2 tablespoons of olive oil to a third ovenproof frying pan. Season the fish on both sides with salt and a pinch or two of cayenne. Turn the heat to high and place the fish in the pan. A minute later, put the fish in

the oven. When the fish browns on one side – about 4 minutes later – turn it over to finish cooking. It will be done about 3 minutes later. (You can test for doneness with a skewer or thin-bladed knife; inserted into the middle, it will meet little or no resistance.) Place the tomato confit in the oven as well, just for a minute.

7 To serve, place a couple of the courgette ribbons on each of 4 plates, along with a few potato slices. Top with a piece of the fish and a few tomatoes. Spread a little tapenade on the fish, and place a little scoop of it on the side. Drizzle the courgette cooking juices over all.

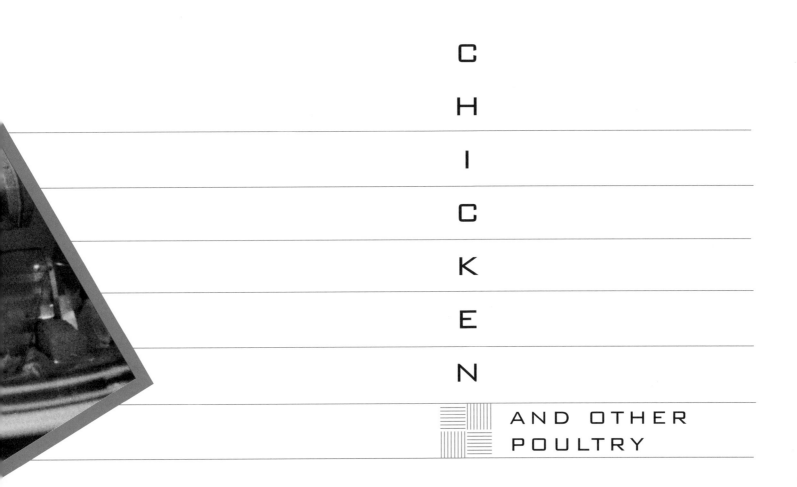

CHICKEN

AND OTHER POULTRY

All of Jean-Georges's chicken sautés border on being braises – they're never covered, but they cook in some liquid. The result is crisp but moist chicken, imbued with all the flavours that surround it. This one, seasoned with ginger, real licorice (page 189) and sweet wine, is among my favourites.

SERVES 4   Red Cabbage and Watercress Salad (page 45) goes well with this.

SAUTÉED CHICKEN WITH LICORICE AND GINGER

2 tablespoons olive oil

1 tablespoon butter

One 1.5kg/3lb chicken, cut up for sautéing (page 193)

Salt and freshly ground black pepper

1 medium carrot, diced into 5-mm/¼-in cubes

2 large shallots, minced

4 large shiitake mushrooms, tops only (use the stems for stock or discard), roughly chopped

5-cm/2-in piece of ginger, minced

1 small piece licorice stick (available at Asian markets), roughly chopped, then ground to a powder in a food mill

¼ tablespoon amchur (sour mango powder) or 1 teaspoon lemon juice

6 baby carrots, peeled, or 1 medium carrot, peeled and cut into strips

150ml/5fl oz white port or sweet white wine

250ml/9fl oz Dark Chicken Stock (page 196) or any chicken stock

Lemon juice

1   Preheat the oven to 250°C/475°F/gas 9. Place the oil and butter in a heavy casserole and turn the heat to high. Season the chicken on both sides with salt and pepper.

2   When the butter foam subsides, add the chicken, skin side down, and brown well on both sides, for a total of 8 to 10 minutes, turning once.

3   When the chicken is browned, tuck the minced vegetables, mushrooms and ginger underneath it and dust the top with ½ teaspoon licorice powder and the amchur powder or lemon juice. Top with the baby carrots or carrot strips.

4   Add the port or wine and cook for 1 minute, then add the stock and transfer the uncovered casserole to the oven. Roast for 5 minutes, then remove the breast and wing-breast pieces; place them on a warm platter. Roast for another 10 minutes, then remove the casserole from the oven and place on top of the stove; return the white meat to the pot.

5   Cook for 1 minute over high heat, then taste and add more salt and pepper if necessary. Sprinkle with enough lemon juice to balance the sweetness of the licorice, about a tablespoon, and serve.

Another of Jean-Georges's wonderful chicken sautés, this one is rich, syrupy, sweet and elegant. Best with fresh figs, but you can make it with dried ones as well; soak them in the port while the chicken is browning.

Serve this, if you like, with Caramelised Beetroots and Turnips (page 128).

SERVES 4

SAUTÉED CHICKEN WITH FIGS

One 1.5kg/3lb chicken, cut up for sautéing (page 193)

Salt and freshly ground black pepper

2 teaspoons sugar

1 tablespoon butter

2 tablespoons olive oil

10-cm/4-in piece of cinnamon stick, broken in 2

1 teaspoon cardamom pods or ½ teaspoon ground cardamom

2 large shallots, minced

4 tablespoons red wine vinegar

125ml/4fl oz port

4 ripe figs, left whole

125ml/4fl oz Dark Chicken Stock (page 196) or any chicken stock

1　Preheat the oven to 250°C/475°F/gas 9. Season the chicken well on both sides with salt and pepper, then sprinkle the skin side with 1 teaspoon of sugar.

2　Combine the butter and olive oil in a large casserole and turn the heat to high. When the butter foam subsides, place the chicken, skin side down, in the pot. Sprinkle the other side with the remaining 1 teaspoon of sugar. Brown the chicken on one side – this will happen faster than usual because of the sugar – then turn over and cook for another minute. Add the cinnamon, cardamom and shallots and cook, stirring a little, for 2 minutes.

3　Add the vinegar. When it has almost evaporated, add the port and the figs. Cook for 2 more minutes, then add the chicken stock and place the un-covered pot in the oven.

4　Roast for 5 minutes, then remove the wing-breast and breast pieces to a warm platter. Roast for another 10 minutes, and return the breast meat to the pot, and place the pot on top of the stove over medium heat. Stir, then adjust the seasoning by adding more vinegar, salt, and/or pepper, as necessary. Serve.

With bacon, dried fruit and potatoes, this is a chicken dish reminiscent of Jean-Georges's Alsatian child-hood, yet it's a dish worthy of attention today.

SERVES 4   Fennel and Apple Salad with Juniper (page 48) sets this off nicely.

 # SAUTÉED CHICKEN WITH PRUNES

125g/4oz piece of bacon

2 tablespoons butter

2 tablespoons extra-virgin olive oil

One 1.5kg/3lb chicken, cut up for sautéing (page 193)

Salt and freshly ground black pepper

4 garlic cloves, lightly crushed

Several thyme sprigs

250g/8oz pitted prunes

500g/1lb waxy, 'new' potatoes, peeled, cut into 2–2.5-cm/¾–1-in chunks, and washed to remove excess starch

300ml/10fl oz Dark Chicken Stock (page 196) or other chicken stock

1 Cut the bacon into 1.2-cm/½-in chunks, then place in a pot with cold water to cover. Bring to the boil, rinse in cold water, and drain. Preheat the oven to 230°C/475°F/gas 9.

2 Turn the heat to high under a flameproof casserole; a minute later, add the butter and oil. Season the chicken on both sides with salt and pepper. When the butter melts, add the chicken, skin side down; tuck the garlic, thyme and bacon amid the chicken pieces.

3 Cook the chicken until nicely browned, then turn over and cook for 2 minutes more. Scatter the prunes and potatoes over the top; add the stock. Bring to the boil and place the uncovered pot in the oven.

4 Remove the white meat pieces when they're cooked through, 5 to 10 minutes later. Cook for another 10 minutes or so, or until all the chicken is nicely browned and cooked through and the potatoes are tender. Return the white meat to the pot to reheat for a moment, then serve.

Jean-Georges developed this dish after a holiday in Morocco, and its flavour is certainly evocative of North Africa. This sauce can be used with sautéed boneless, skinless chicken breasts. But try it this way if you can - the sauce combines beautifully with the crisp skin of the chicken.

Simmered Carrots with Cumin and Orange (page 130) set this dish off nicely.

SERVES 4

SAUTÉED CHICKEN WITH GREEN OLIVES AND CORIANDER

2 tablespoons plus 1 teaspoon extra virgin olive oil

50g/2oz minced onion

2 teaspoons minced ginger

5-cm/2-in piece cinnamon

A few strands of saffron or ½ teaspoon dried turmeric

Salt

470ml/16fl oz Rich Chicken Stock (page 195) or other stock

2 tablespoons peanut or neutral-flavoured oil, such as sunflower

One 1.5–2kg/3–4lb chicken, cut up for sautéing (page 193)

Freshly ground black pepper

2 tablespoons minced green olives

2 teaspoons lemon juice

1 tablespoon coarsely chopped coriander leaves

1 Preheat the oven to 230°C/475°F/gas 9. Place 2 tablespoons of olive oil in a small saucepan over medium heat. Add the onion, ginger, cinnamon, saffron or turmeric, and a pinch of salt and cook, stirring occasionally, for about 5 minutes. Add the stock and increase the heat to high; cook, stirring occasionally, while you prepare the chicken. When the liquid has reduced by about three-quarters and becomes syrupy, turn off the heat.

2 Heat the peanut oil in a large, preferably nonstick, ovenproof frying pan over medium-high heat for a minute or two. Season the chicken on both sides with salt and pepper. Place the chicken in the pan, skin side down, and cook undisturbed until lightly browned, for 5 to 8 minutes. Turn over and cook on the other side for about 2 minutes. Turn over so the skin is down again, and place the pan in the oven. Check it after 15 minutes, and remove the pieces as they are cooked through (the breasts will be cooked before the legs; keep them warm).

3 When the chicken is just about done, finish the sauce: Stir in the remaining 1 teaspoon of olive oil, the olives and some salt (not too much – the olives are salty) and pepper. Cook for about 2 minutes over medium-high heat, stirring once or twice. Turn off the heat and add the lemon juice and coriander. Remove the cinnamon stick.

4 To serve, arrange the chicken on 4 plates. Spoon the sauce around it, not over it, so the chicken stays crunchy.

A Vong standard, in which you make a powerful marinade, then wrap the halves of a whole boned chicken around it. The next day, you do the cooking – which is the easy part. The results are beyond divine. Serve this with Sticky Rice Steamed in Banana Leaves (page 145) and Peppery Green Beans (page 127).

I've left the serving size vague intentionally, because although few of us eat half of a chicken at one sitting, most people seem to be able to polish off that amount once it's boned. Instructions for boning a chicken are given opposite, or just ask your butcher to do it for you.

SERVES 2 – 4

CHICKEN WITH LEMONGRASS

2 stalks lemongrass, trimmed, outer leaves peeled off to expose the tender inner core, and thinly sliced

2 large shallots, roughly chopped

2 garlic cloves, roughly chopped

1 fresh red chilli, roughly chopped, or 1 teaspoon dried red chilli flakes

1 tablespoon nam pla or nuoc mam (Asian fish sauce)

One 1.5–2kg/3–4lb chicken, wing tips removed

Salt and freshly ground black pepper

2 tablespoons vegetable, grapeseed or other neutral-flavoured oil

1 Combine the lemongrass, shallots, garlic, chilli, and nam pla in a food processor and purée roughly, stopping the machine to scrape down the sides once or twice. If possible, do this the day before you want to serve the chicken.

2 To bone the chicken, see opposite. Trim the chicken of excess fat and use a sharp knife to score the dark meat a little so it will cook as quickly as the white meat. (Alternatively, you may cut up the chicken as for a sauté; use the recipe for Sautéed Chicken with Licorice and Ginger on page 86 for guidance in timing.)

3 Spread the marinade all over the inside of the chicken, but none at all on the skin. Press it into the flesh a little bit. Sprinkle with salt and pepper and fold the chicken over onto itself. Season the outside with salt and pepper. If you have the time, wrap it in plastic and rest for several hours, refrigerated. If not possible, proceed.

4 Preheat the oven to 250°C/475°F/gas 9. Place the oil in a large, nonstick, ovenproof pan set over high heat. When the oil is hot, place the chicken in the pan.

5 When the chicken begins to brown, 3 or 4 minutes later, put the pan in the oven. Cook for about 10 minutes, or until the bottom is crisp, then turn over the chicken and return the pan to the oven for another 7 minutes or so, again until crisp. Turn once more and cook for another minute. Check for doneness–there should be no traces of pink – and serve.

NOTE:

To bone a chicken: Start with a sharp boning (thin-bladed) knife. Cut off the wings where they meet the breast. (Save them and other scraps you accumulate for stock.) Turn the bird so the breast is face up. Make a cut along the entire length of the breastbone, to one side or the other. Cut down with the point of the knife, following the ribs, until you've completely removed half the bird – breast, wing and leg-thigh – from the carcass. At this point the breast is already boned. Repeat the process on the other side of the bird.

The thigh bone is easily exposed: just cut around it until nothing is holding it to the chicken except the joint with the leg bone. Now cut around the leg bone and remove both in one piece. What you have now may look a little like a mess, but it is in fact half of a boned chicken; repeat on the other side and proceed with the recipe.

This recipe uses the same technique as the previous one, but with Indian rather than Thai seasonings. There's another difference, too: this dish does not really benefit from marinating, so there's no need for thinking ahead.

Serve it, if you like, with Curried Artichokes (page 126) and Tamarind Ketchup (page 200).

SERVES 4

 # OVEN-CRISPED CHICKEN WITH FRAGRANT SPICES

1 tablespoon cumin seeds

1 whole nutmeg

1 tablespoon coriander seeds

1 tablespoon star anise

1/2 tablespoon cloves

1/2 tablespoon freshly ground black pepper

One 1.5–2kg/3–4lb chicken, wing tips removed

Salt

2 tablespoons vegetable, grapeseed or other neutral-flavoured oil

1 Combine the cumin, nutmeg, coriander, star anise, cloves and pepper in a dry frying pan and turn the heat to medium-high. Cook, shaking the pan occasionally, until the mixture is fragrant, 1 to 2 minutes. Grind the mixture to a coarse powder in a coffee or spice grinder or in a pestle and mortar. (You can store this mixture in an opaque container for up to a year.) Preheat the oven to 250°C/475°F/gas 9.

2 To bone the chicken, see Note, page 91. Trim the chicken of excess fat and use a sharp knife to score the dark meat a little so it will cook as quickly as the white meat. (Alternatively, you may cut up the chicken as for a sauté; use the recipe for Sautéed Chicken with Licorice and Ginger on page 86 for guidance in timing.)

3 Sprinkle each side of the chicken with salt and about 1/2 teaspoon of the spice mixture. Place the oil in a large, nonstick ovenproof frying pan set over high heat. When the oil is hot, place the chicken in the pan.

4 When the chicken begins to brown, 3 or 4 minutes later, put the pan in the oven. Cook for about 8 minutes, or until the bottom is crisp, then turn the chicken over and return the pan to the oven for another 5 minutes or so, again until the chicken is crisp. Turn once more and cook for another minute. Check for doneness – there should be no traces of pink – and serve.

That's right, just cloves. Although the chicken is broiled, it simultaneously poaches in the cream, becoming moist and rich.

SERVES 4

Serve with Glazed Autumn Vegetables and Fruits (page 137) or any salad. Note that this dish must 'marinate' overnight.

GRILLED CHICKEN BREAST WITH CLOVES

16 cloves

4 boneless, skinless chicken breasts (or guinea hen or pheasant), about 500–600g/1–1¼lb

190ml/6fl oz cream

Salt and freshly ground black pepper

1 Place the cloves in the smallest saucepan you have and cover with water. Bring to the boil, drain and rinse. Repeat 4 more times.

2 Pierce each of the breast pieces with 4 cloves. Wrap in clingfilm and refrigerate overnight.

3 Preheat the grill and adjust the rack so that it is about 8cm/3in from the heat source. Place the breasts in a roasting dish just large enough to accommodate them. Pour the cream over and around them and sprinkle with salt and pepper.

4 Grill for 3 to 4 minutes per side, until the breasts firm up and become spotted with brown. Remove the cloves and serve the breasts with the remaining cream (much of it will have been absorbed) spooned over them.

As simple and elegant a weeknight dish as you could wish. If you can get fresh pine shoots – the tender ends of the needles of the white pine tree – by all means use them. The idea is that you dip each piece of chicken in a pine shoot–hazelnut–salt mixture before you eat.

Otherwise, substitute fresh rosemary leaves and serve with Caramelised Beetroots and Turnips (page 128).

SERVES 4

ROAST CHICKEN BREASTS WITH PINE OR ROSEMARY

4 boneless chicken breast halves, preferably with skin on

Salt and freshly ground black pepper

3 tablespoons vegetable, grapeseed or other neutral-flavoured oil

1 tablespoon very finely minced pine shoot needles or rosemary leaves

About 1 teaspoon coarse sea salt

2 tablespoons very finely minced hazelnuts

125ml/4fl oz Rich Chicken Stock (page 195) or other chicken stock

1 Preheat the oven to 250°C/475°F/gas 9. Sprinkle the chicken on both sides with salt and pepper. Place the oil in a large ovenproof frying pan over high heat. When it begins to smoke, add the chicken, skin side down. Cook for about 3 minutes, until nicely browned, then turn the chicken over and put the frying pan in the oven for another 3 minutes or so, until done.

2 While the chicken is cooking, mix the pine shoots or rosemary leaves with the coarse sea salt and the hazelnuts. Divide this mixture onto each of 4 plates.

3 When the chicken is done, place a piece on each of the plates. Add the stock to the frying pan and cook over high heat, stirring, for just a minute, until reduced by about half. Spoon a little of this juice over each breast and serve.

This fast weeknight stir-fry is finished with a beautiful glaze of tamarind, the exotic sweet-and-sour flavour of which is immediately appealing. Jean-Georges makes this with chicken or veal at Vong, but it's also good with pork.

SERVES 4

Serve with plain rice or Sticky Rice Steamed in Banana Leaves (page 145) and something light, such as Beetroot and Ginger Salad (page 42) or Cucumber Salad with Lemongrass (page 46).

STIR-FRIED CHICKEN WITH TAMARIND GLAZE

2 tablespoons vegetable, grapeseed or other neutral-flavoured oil

500g/1lb boneless, skinless chicken breast, veal or pork, cut into 2.5cm/1in cubes

Salt and freshly ground black pepper

1 teaspoon sugar

125g/4oz shiitake mushrooms, stems removed and discarded or reserved for stock

50g/2oz sliced shallots

2 teaspoons minced garlic

2 tablespoons tamarind purée (see Note)

125g/4oz bean sprouts

1 small fresh chilli, minced, about 1 teaspoon

12–15 chopped Thai or other basil leaves

1 Place the oil in a large, heavy frying pan and turn the heat to high. While it is heating, sprinkle the meat with salt, pepper and sugar.

2 Add the meat to the frying pan. Cook, undisturbed, for 2 minutes, then add the mushrooms, shallots and garlic, and stir. Continue to cook over the highest possible heat for another 2 minutes or so, then add the tamarind purée and 2 tablespoons of water. Toss for a minute.

3 Stir in the bean sprouts, chilli, and basil. Taste, adjust seasoning and serve.

NOTE:

To make tamarind purée, place 500g/1lb tamarind pulp (available at Asian markets) in a saucepan with 250ml/9fl oz water and turn the heat to medium. Cook, whisking lightly to break up the lumps, and add more water whenever the mixture becomes dry, until you've added a total of about 470ml/16fl oz. The process will take about 10 minutes; the result will be quite thick, but fairly smooth. Put the tamarind through a food mill; you will have about 250ml/9fl oz of purée.

A butter-basted bird with a quick traditional stuffing may not seem in keeping with the rest of Jean-Georges's repertoire. But it's a dish he loves to make (it was one of the first specials at Restaurant Jean-Georges) and one he loves to eat. This amount of stuffing is enough for two Cornish hens or poussins (baby chickens), or one larger chicken or guinea hen.

Jean-Georges sometimes uses pork belly in place of olive oil to sauté the livers. To do so, mince 50g/2oz pork belly and render it over medium-high heat in the frying pan before adding the livers, then proceed.

You don't need much of a side dish here; try Dip 'n' Eat Broccoli (page 129) or Fresh Pea Pancake (page 133).

SERVES 4

ROAST POUSSINS WITH HERB-BREAD STUFFING

50g/2oz good bread (about 4 slices), crusts removed

4 tablespoons extra virgin olive oil

125g/4oz chicken livers, diced

Salt and freshly ground black pepper

3 garlic cloves, minced

1 large shallot, minced

1 teaspoon thyme leaves

2 tablespoons minced parsley leaves

2 poussins, about 500g/1lb each, rinsed and dried

15g/½oz butter

2 thyme sprigs

2 garlic cloves, unpeeled and lightly crushed

1 Preheat the oven to 250°C/475°F/gas 9. Cut the bread into 1.2cm/½in cubes. Place 2 tablespoons of the olive oil in a frying pan and turn the heat to high. A minute later, add the bread. Toss it until it is golden brown, about 5 minutes, then place it in a bowl.

2 Wipe out the pan. Add 1 tablespoon of olive oil and turn the heat to high. Sprinkle the livers liberally with salt and pepper, then toss in the pan. Immediately add the minced garlic, shallot and thyme. Cook, stirring occasionally, just until the liver loses its rawness. Add to the bread and toss with the parsley and lots of salt and pepper. (You may prepare the stuffing in advance; refrigerate, in a covered container, for up to 2 days.)

3 When the stuffing is cool enough to handle, stuff the birds. Truss them if you like, or simply close their rear vents with skewers to keep the stuffing from falling out. Season them all over with salt and pepper.

4 Place an ovenproof casserole over high heat and add the remaining olive oil, along with the butter. Immediately add the thyme sprigs, garlic cloves and any scraps from the birds, such as the necks or wing tips. Add the birds and brown lightly on both sides of the breast, then turn the birds onto their backs and place the pan in the oven.

5 Spoon the pan juices over the birds every 5 or 10 minutes. When they are done – after about 30 minutes of roasting (there should be no traces of pink) – put them on a platter. Remove the thyme sprigs, garlic and grease from the pan. Place the pan over high heat and add 90ml/3fl oz water; cook for a minute, scraping up all of the brown bits from the bottom of the pan. When they are incorporated, pour the *jus* over the birds. Carve and serve.

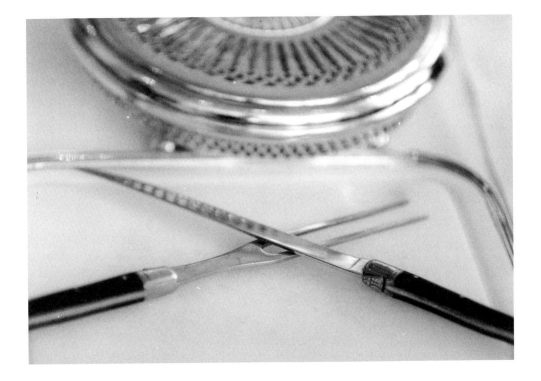

It's not clear which part of the recipe is the star here: the meltingly tender onion compôte, which should cook for at least 30 minutes, or the exotically seasoned bird. You can use chickens, poussin, or pigeon. Chickens are the largest of the three birds, but pigeon the richest. The only adjustment you'll need to make is in cooking time; pigeon should be grilled for 6 minutes (for rare pigeon) to 10 minutes (for medium-to-well-done pigeon); poussin for about 9 minutes, chicken for at least 12-15.

If you choose to serve this with greens – a good option – use the cooking juices from the birds to mix in with your salad dressing. It all goes nicely with Pan-Fried Noodle Cake (page 144).

SERVES 4

CHICKEN WITH ONION COMPOTE

5 tablespoons butter

3 large onions, sliced

Salt

2 tablespoons minced fresh red chilli

1 tablespoon lemon juice

4 portions chicken or 4 poussins or pigeon

Freshly ground black pepper

1/4 teaspoon ground cumin

1/4 teaspoon ground ginger

1/4 teaspoon All-Purpose Curry Powder (page 214) or any curry powder

1/4 teaspoon ground cinnamon

1 Place 4 tablespoons of the butter in a frying pan and turn the heat to medium-high. When it melts, add the onions and a large pinch of salt. Cook, stirring frequently, until the onions are coated with butter, then reduce the heat to low.

2 Add the minced chilli, cover, and continue to cook, stirring only occasionally, until the onions are very, very soft, for at least 30 minutes. Season with the lemon juice.

3 Meanwhile, divide the birds into semi-boneless halves by cutting down along (not through) the breastbones of each, and through the joint where the thigh attaches to the carcass.

4 Preheat the grill and set the rack 10–15cm/4–6in from the heat source. Use the remaining 1 tablespoon of butter to grease the bottom of a roasting pan. Season both sides of the birds with salt and pepper and place on a baking tray, skin side up. Combine the cumin, ginger, curry powder and cinnamon and set aside.

5 Grill the birds until the skin is brown and crisp and the bird rare (for pigeon, about 6 minutes) to well done (for poussin or chicken, 9 minutes or longer). You may need to move chicken pieces a little farther from the heat in order to cook them through without burning the skin, but you will not if they are small.

6 Leave the birds rest for a minute or two, then sprinkle them on both sides with a pinch of the spice mixture. Mix their juices in with the cooked onions, or over an assortment of greens, which is good with this dish. Place a spoonful of the onions in the centre of each plate and surround with pieces of the birds.

CHICKEN AND OTHER POULTRY

99

Jean-George's version of duck a l'orange isn't the traditional, gooey, overly sweet one. The effort goes into the accompanying sauce; the duck itself takes just ten minutes to cook. Make every effort to use duck bones for the stock, even if it means freezing spare parts over a period of weeks or even months; the resulting flavour is complex beyond belief. (See the following recipe, Braised Duck and Vegetables with Asian Spices, if you're looking for a good use for duck legs.)

Choose either Corn Cake (page 142) or Millet Cake (page 143) for a side dish.

SERVES 4 GENEROUSLY

DUCK À LA JOJO

3 teaspoons vegetable, grapeseed or other neutral-flavoured oil

500g/1lb duck bones: wing and leg tips, necks, breastbones and scraps

1 cinnamon stick

1 tablespoon coriander seeds

1 tablespoon mace pieces or ground mace

1 tablespoon ground ginger

1 medium onion, roughly chopped

1 celery stalk, roughly chopped

1 carrot, peeled and roughly chopped

2 tablespoons golden syrup

2 tablespoons honey

4 tablespoons sherry vinegar

4 tablespoons orange juice

2 tablespoons lemon juice

1 Preheat the oven to 250°C/475°F/gas 9. Place a heavy ovenproof frying pan over high heat for a minute, then add 2 teaspoons of oil and the bones. Transfer immediately to the oven. Brown the bones, turning the pieces occasionally, until very brown and crisp, about 30 minutes.

2 Meanwhile, toast the cinnamon stick, coriander seeds and mace pieces (do not toast ground mace) in a dry frying pan over medium heat, shaking the pan occasionally for about a minute, or until it becomes aromatic. Add the ground ginger and, if you're using it, the ground mace. Remove from the heat and leave to cool. Break up the cinnamon stick, then grind the spices to a powder in a coffee grinder or pestle and mortar.

3 When the bones are well browned, add the onion, celery and carrot to them and stir. Sprinkle with 1 teaspoon of the spice mixture and return to the oven until the vegetables begin to brown, for about 5 minutes.

4 Place the bone-and-vegetable mixture in a sieve and drain out and discard the fat. Return the bone mixture to the frying pan and add the golden syrup and honey. Return the frying pan to the oven for 7 or 8 minutes, until the vegetables are nicely browned. Everything will be sticking to the pan, but don't worry about it. Do not turn off the oven.

5 Add the sherry vinegar, orange juice and lemon juice to the frying pan and stir. Then add the stock and/or water; it should be just enough to almost

470ml/16fl oz Rich Chicken Stock (page 195), or other stock or water, or a combination

4 boneless duck breasts with their skin on, about 175g/6oz each

Salt and freshly ground black pepper

1 tablespoon butter

1 tablespoon lime juice

cover the bones. Cook over medium-high heat; the mixture should be bubbling, but not furiously. As it cooks, the liquid will darken and thicken slightly as a result of the spices.

6 Simmer for 30 to 40 minutes, or until reduced by a little more than half; you want to end up with about 250ml/9fl oz of liquid. Strain. (You may prepare the recipe in advance up to this point; refrigerate the broth in a covered container for up to 2 days.)

7 Season the duck breasts with salt and more of the spice mixture, about ¼ teaspoon per side of each breast; press the spices into the skin a bit.

8 Place the remaining 1 teaspoon of oil in a large, heavy ovenproof frying pan and turn the heat to medium-high. Add the duck, skin side down. After 1 minute, when it begins to brown, place it in the still-hot oven. Cook until the skin is very brown and the duck firm, for 7 to 10 minutes. Remove the pan from the oven, turn the duck over and place the pan on a burner over high heat for just a minute or two, until the duck is cooked to medium-rare.

9 When the duck is ready, leave it to rest while you finish the sauce. Add salt and pepper to the broth, along with the butter and lime juice. Taste and correct the seasoning. Slice the duck and serve it with a bit of the sauce spooned over. Garnish with a tiny sprinkling of the spice mixture.

The best way to serve this Asian duck confit is to let the duck cool to room temperature, then take it off the bone and place it on a bed of greens, or reheat it and serve with white rice (especially Sticky Rice Steamed in Banana Leaves, page 145). Despite the long cooking time, with no added liquid, the duck legs remain moist and become tender from the aromatic steam created by the cooking vegetables.

Note that this dish uses only duck legs. Use the breasts for the preceding recipe – Duck à la JoJo – reserving all bones, wing tips, leg ends and other scraps for that stock.

SERVES 4

BRAISED DUCK AND VEGETABLES WITH ASIAN SPICES

1 medium onion, minced

1 celery stalk, minced

1 carrot, minced

1/2 stalk lemongrass, peeled, trimmed to expose its tender inner core, and very finely minced

2 tablespoons plus 2 teaspoons minced ginger

2 tablespoons vegetable, grapeseed or other neutral-flavoured oil

6 duck legs, excess fat removed, bony ends hacked off and reserved for stock

Salt

2 teaspoons 5-spice powder

1 spring onion, minced

Soy sauce

1 Preheat the oven to 180°C/350°F/gas 4. Make a bed of the vegetables, lemongrass and 2 tablespoons of ginger in a heavy ovenproof frying pan. Drizzle with the oil.

2 Sprinkle the duck legs with salt and 5-spice powder on both sides. Place the duck legs on top of the vegetables, skin side up. Roast for 2 hours, undisturbed.

3 Remove the frying pan from the oven and leave it to cool. Remove the meat from the bones; discard the skin and bones and shred the meat with your fingers. Combine it with the cooked vegetables, the spring onion and the remaining 2 teaspoons of ginger. Season to taste with salt or soy sauce. Serve the meat over rice or on a bed of greens.

Quail, a meaty litle bird that is fun to eat, can be insipid-tasting, but not when it's drenched with this big-flavoured marinade. Use the same procedure for poussins, chicken pieces, or pigeon; adjust cooking times accordingly.

These are great surrounding a mound of Red Cabbage and Water-cress Salad (page 45).

SERVES 4

MARINATED QUAIL, VONG-STYLE

50g/2oz minced shallots

1 tablespoon minced ginger

2 tablespoons palm or brown sugar

1 tablespoon minced garlic

1 tablespoon cracked black peppercorns

2 tablespoons 5-spice powder

4 tablespoons rice vinegar

250ml/9fl oz soy sauce

6 quail

Vegetable, grapeseed or other neutral-flavoured oil

1　Combine the shallots, ginger, sugar, garlic, peppercorns, 5-spice powder, vinegar, soy sauce and 250ml/9fl oz water in a medium saucepan and bring to the boil, stirring. Cool.

2　Cut along each side of the breastbone of each bird, then straight down through where the thigh meets the body; you will obtain 2 semi-boneless halves from each bird.

3　Strain the cooled marinade, then combine with the quail in a large bowl. Marinate for at least 3 hours, but no more than 24 hours.

4　When you're ready to cook, drain the quail of the marinade. Place 2 table-spoons of oil in one or more large frying pans and turn the heat to high. Sauté the quail, skin side down, until nicely browned, for about 4 minutes. Turn over and brown the other side for 2 minutes, or until the quail are cooked through. Serve hot.

Old-fashioned confit recipes call for long marinating times, plenty of duck fat and long, gentle cooking. While duck fat is still welcome in Jean-Georges's kitchens, he also likes a light confit made with olive oil (this need not be your best estate-bottled extra virgin olive oil).

He serves it with salad greens and a dressing based on a quickly made juice from the meat scraps. This confit can be made with chicken or rabbit.

SERVES 4

CHICKEN CONFIT WITH SALAD

One 1.5kg/3lb chicken or rabbit, skin removed

Coarse sea salt

1 tablespoon vegetable, grapeseed or other neutral-flavoured oil

½ carrot, peeled and chopped

½ celery stalk, chopped

1 shallot, minced

3 garlic cloves

2 thyme sprigs, or ¼ teaspoon dried thyme

Olive oil, rendered duck fat or rendered chicken fat as needed

4 thin slices French bread

About 4 tablespoons extra virgin olive oil

125g/4oz shelled fava or lima beans (frozen are okay)

About 1 tablespoon sherry vinegar

Salt and freshly ground black pepper

6 handfuls mesclun or other mixed greens

16 black olives, such as Niçoise

1 teaspoon fresh thyme leaves, optional

1 If you are using a chicken, cut the breast into 4 pieces and the legs into 2 pieces; set all the other pieces aside. If you are using a rabbit, cut the saddle into 4 pieces and the back legs into 2 pieces; set all the other pieces aside. Sprinkle the breast and legs or saddle and back legs with about 1 tablespoon coarse sea salt and leave to sit for 30 minutes.

2 Meanwhile, put a deep frying pan or broad saucepan over medium-high heat for 2 or 3 minutes, then add the 1 tablespoon of oil, followed by the unsalted meat. Brown the meat over medium-high heat for about 5 minutes, shaking the pan occasionally and turning over the meat once. Add the carrot, celery and shallot. Smash 2 of the garlic cloves and add them, together with the thyme. Still over medium-high heat, continue to brown the meat for another 3 to 5 minutes, shaking the pan occasionally. Add 470ml/16fl oz of water, all at once. When the water boils, reduce the heat so that the mixture bubbles, but not too rapidly.

3 After 20 minutes, the liquid will be reduced to about 250m/9fl oz; strain it into a small saucepan (discard the bones and vegetables) and cook over medium-high heat for about 15 minutes, or until it is reduced to a scant half. The reduction will be quite thick, almost syrupy, very dark and intensely flavoured. Set aside.

4 When the salted meat has rested for 30 minutes, place it in a saucepan just large enough to fit it comfortably. Cover with olive oil or melted chicken or duck fat; little or none of the meat should be exposed to the air. Set the heat to medium-high and adjust it so that just a few bubbles come up. Use an instant-read or frying thermometer and keep the oil at about 100°C/200°F,

no higher. You do not want the meat to brown at all. Alternatively, cover the saucepan and place it in an oven preheated to 100°C/200°F/gas ¼.

5 Cook the meat, turning over once or twice, for 2 hours. Remove the meat and drain it briefly. The olive oil or other fat can be set aside and used for sautéing or stir-frying. (You may prepare the recipe in advance up to this point; refrigerate the meat and stock separately, well-wrapped or in covered containers, for up to several days.)

6 Sprinkle the bread with a little olive oil, then grill it until lightly browned on both sides. Cut the remaining garlic clove in half and rub the bread all over with it.

7 Put a small pot of water on to boil and add the beans. About 10 minutes later, when they're tender, drain and plunge the beans into iced water to stop them cooking. Drain again.

8 Make a vinaigrette by combining the reduced bone broth, extra virgin olive oil, vinegar, salt and pepper; taste and adjust seasoning as necessary. Reheat the meat if necessary: you can either cook it in a frying pan for a few minutes or just warm it in a 150°C/300°F/gas 2 oven (or even in a microwave); it should be warm, not hot.

9 Divide the greens among 4 plates. Top each with 2 pieces of the confit, then a scattering of olives and beans. Place a toasted slice of French bread on top, then a grating of pepper, a little salt and a few thyme leaves, if you have them. Dress with a couple of tablespoons of the vinaigrette and serve.

This slow-cooked stew is one of those flavour-packed dishes in which none of the ingredients loses its identity but all contribute to a mighty total.

Making it is a lengthy process, but hardly a difficult one; start it the day before you want to eat it, and serve it with plenty of white rice (especially Sticky Rice Steamed in Banana Leaves, page 145). There is a lot of sauce here, and it's all worth eating.

SERVES 4

RABBIT CURRY

3 stalks lemongrass, trimmed and chopped, the trimmings reserved

3 small fresh chillies, trimmed and chopped

2 large shallots, chopped

2 tablespoons turmeric

1 tablespoon All-Purpose Curry Powder (page 214) or use commercial curry powder

1 tablespoon curry paste or another tablespoon of curry powder

2 tablespoons nam pla or nuoc mam (Asian fish sauce)

1 tablespoon sugar

One 1.5kg/3lb rabbit or chicken, cut into serving pieces

3 tablespoons vegetable, grapeseed or other neutral-flavoured oil

1 large onion, sliced

125ml/4fl oz chopped tomatoes (canned are fine; don't bother to drain)

1 Wrap the lemongrass trimmings in a cheesecloth bag and refrigerate. Combine the chopped lemongrass, chillies, shallots, 1 tablespoon of turmeric, the curry powder, curry paste, nam pla and sugar in a food processor and process, stopping the machine and scraping down the sides if necessary, until it becomes a paste. This will take a couple of minutes, because lemongrass takes a while to break down.

2 Toss the rabbit with about half the paste mixture, then cover it and refrigerate it overnight. Cover and refrigerate the remaining paste as well.

3 About 2½ hours before serving, place 1 tablespoon of oil in a deep casserole and turn the heat to medium-high. Add the onion and the remaining paste mixture and cook, stirring, until the onion is slightly softened, for about 5 minutes.

4 Meanwhile, place the remaining 2 tablespoons of oil in a large frying pan and turn the heat to medium-high. Brown the rabbit carefully on both sides – in batches if necessary (add a little more oil if you need to) – taking care not to burn the skin. As the pieces brown, transfer them to the casserole.

5 When all the meat has been browned and transferred to the casserole, add the tomatoes, lemongrass trimmings (in their cheesecloth bag), chicken stock and remaining 1 tablespoon of turmeric. Bring to the boil, uncovered, then adjust the heat so it cooks at a steady simmer until the meat is tender; at least 1½ hours (chicken will take less time, but still at least 1 hour). Taste and add salt if necessary, but remember that nam pla is very salty.

1.4l/2⅓ pints Rich Chicken Stock
(page 195) or any chicken stock

Salt

1 can (about 400ml/14fl oz)
unsweetened coconut milk

1 tablespoon lime juice

6 When the meat is very tender, almost falling off the bone, add the coconut milk and cook for another 10 minutes. Remove the rabbit to a platter or bowl, and remove the lemongrass bundle and discard.

7 Carefully purée the sauce, preferably with a hand-held blender. Taste it and add the lime juice and salt, if necessary. Spoon over the meat and serve, with white rice.

M

E

A

T

The basis of this rich stew – a combination of French pot-au-feu and Vietnamese pho – is a classic beef stock seasoned with far-from-classic ingredients, among them ginger, lemongrass, cinnamon and chilli. At Vong, Jean-Georges finishes it with noodles, a grilled steak and some blanched green vegetables; I have done it that way at home, but have also doubled the amount of noodles and omitted the steak entirely.

No side dish is needed here. Start, if you like, with Rice Paper Rolls of Shrimps and Herbs (page 14) or a simple salad, such as Fennel and Apple Salad with Juniper (page 48).

SERVES 6

BEEF WITH GINGER

2.5kg/5lb assorted beef bones, such as marrow bones, shin and oxtail

250g/8oz piece of ginger, split in half (don't bother to peel)

1 large onion, split in half (don't bother to peel)

1 whole garlic bulb, cut in half through its equator

2 stalks lemongrass, trimmed and bruised all over with the back of a knife

8 star anise

15-cm/6-in piece of cinnamon stick

2 dried red chilli peppers

One 5-cm/2-in piece of ginger, peeled and finely julienned

250g/8oz linguine-size rice noodles

500g/1lb broccoli and/or other green vegetables, such as snow peas and/or green beans, trimmed as necessary

About 2 tablespoons soy sauce

1 Place the meat bones in a large pot with water to cover – about 5 litres/1 gallon – and bring to the boil. Meanwhile, place the cut side of the ginger and onion in a dry frying pan over high heat and cook until black on that one side; add to the beef pot with the garlic and lemongrass.

2 Toast the anise, cinnamon and chillies in a dry frying pan over medium heat, for about 1 minute, until aromatic. Add those to the stock.

3 When the stock mixture comes to the boil, reduce the heat so that it simmers. Cook for about 3 hours, until the meat falls from the bone. Cool, then strain, pushing on the solids to extract as much liquid as possible from them. Refrigerate for several hours or overnight.

4 About 30 minutes before you're ready to eat, remove most of the fat from the surface of the cold stock and discard. Put the stock in a saucepan and bring it to simmering point; add the julienned ginger.

5 Soak the rice noodles in fairly hot water (about 60°C/120°F, almost too hot to touch) for 10 to 20 minutes, or until soft. Drain thoroughly.

6 Blanch the broccoli or other green vegetables in boiling water to cover, just until tender. Use a slotted spoon to remove them from the water (keep the water simmering) and shock in iced water to stop the cooking.

Six 175g/6oz rump steaks

6 spring onions, trimmed and minced

7 Season the stock to taste with soy sauce.

8 Grill or pan-griddle the steaks until they are done as you like them. Slice, then place the slices in 6 large bowls with a portion of the noodles, then ladle in a portion of the simmering stock. Reheat the vegetables quickly in the simmering water, then drain and add them to the bowls along with the spring onions. Serve immediately.

There are two classic combinations at work here: meat and carrots, and meat and red wine. But the marriage of the two, especially without any meat stock, is unusual. This is an example of a sauce that tastes odd by itself; put it on any grilled meat, though – especially beef and pork – and it shines.

Potato 'Ravioli' (page 4) would be an ideal side dish here and this recipe is so easy that you'll have the time you need for that one.

STEAK WITH RED WINE REDUCTION AND CARROT PUREE

1 bottle red wine (or the leftovers from a couple of recently opened bottles)

6 small or 2 medium-to-large carrots

Salt

750g–1kg/1½–2lb fillet or rump steak or pork chops

1 Start a wood or charcoal fire in a grill or preheat a gas grill.

2 Place the wine in a large saucepan and turn the heat to high. When it begins boiling, reduce the heat just a bit and reduce the wine until there is about 250ml/9fl oz of syrupy wine essence remaining: this takes about 20 minutes.

3 Meanwhile, prepare the carrots: peel and cut them into chunks, then place in a small saucepan with water to cover and a pinch of salt. Cover the pan and cook the carrots over medium heat until tender, for 15 to 20 minutes. Drain, reserving the cooking liquid. Purée the carrots in a blender or food processor, using a bit of their cooking liquid if necessary.

4 Grill the steak(s) to the desired doneness. Place the reduced wine in a bowl and stir about 125ml/4fl oz of the carrot purée into it. If it is too thick, add a teaspoon or more of reserved carrot cooking water. Taste and add salt if necessary; serve with the steak.

'Veal,' says Jean-Georges, 'is so bland that you have to do something exciting to it.' This recipe qualifies: pineapple juice sparked with ginger, cayenne and orange marmalade. It's perfectly acceptable to use canned pineapple juice for this dish, but if you want to use freshly made juice, put about 500g/1lb trimmed and cored pineapple through a juicer before beginning.

This is nice with Curried Artichokes (page 126) or Millet Cake (page 143).

SERVES 4

VEAL CHOPS WITH PINEAPPLE JUICE AND PINE NUTS

50g/2oz pine nuts

2 tablespoons peeled and julienned ginger (do not mince it finely)

375ml/13fl oz pineapple juice

1 teaspoon orange marmalade, preferably the bitter ('Seville') kind

15g/½oz butter

2 tablespoons lemon juice, or more to taste

Salt

Cayenne pepper

4 veal chops

Freshly ground black pepper

2 tablespoons extra virgin olive oil

Minced chives

1 Preheat the oven to 250°C/475°F/gas 9. Place the pine nuts in a small saucepan with water to cover. Bring to the boil and cook for 1 minute. Drain, then immediately plunge into a bowl of iced water. Drain again and set aside.

2 Combine the ginger and pineapple juice in a saucepan and turn the heat to medium-high. Cook, stirring occasionally, until reduced by about half, about 10 minutes. Stir in the marmalade, butter, lemon juice (use more if the marmalade is sweet), salt and cayenne. Taste and adjust seasoning; the mixture should be quite strong. Stir in the pine nuts and keep warm.

3 Sprinkle the chops liberally with salt and pepper. Place the oil in a large ovenproof frying pan and turn the heat to high. A minute later, add the chops. Sear on one side for about 3 minutes; turn over the chops and place the pan in the oven. Roast, turning once or twice, until done (their centres will be barely pink); this takes 10 to 15 minutes depending on the thickness of the chops.

4 Spoon the sauce over the chops, garnish with minced chives and serve.

A striking-looking dish, especially with rare-cooked lamb, which makes it red, black and green. If time allows, the mushroom flavour will be even more pronounced if the mushroom-crusted lamb sits in the refrigerator for about 2 hours before cooking. Any butcher, including those in supermarkets, can provide you with boned racks of lamb, although it is among the easiest boning jobs to do yourself.

SERVES 4

Serve this, if you like, with Beetroot Tartare (page 43) or Warm Potato Salad with Caramelised Shallots and Watercress (page 50).

BONELESS LAMB WITH MUSHROOM CRUST AND LEEK PURÉE

2 leeks, trimmed of hard green parts, split in half, well washed and roughly chopped

1 tablespoon butter

Salt and freshly ground black pepper

50g/2oz dried black trumpet or other dried mushrooms

1 egg, beaten with a little salt and pepper

Flour for dredging

2 racks of lamb, boned

3 tablespoons extra virgin olive oil

125g/4oz shiitake or other mushrooms, trimmed and cut into chunks

2 garlic cloves, lightly smashed

2 thyme sprigs

Coarse sea salt

1 Cook the leeks in boiling salted water, for about 4 minutes, until tender. Drain and transfer to a blender with the butter and salt and pepper to taste. Purée and keep warm.

2 Place the dried mushrooms in a spice or coffee grinder and grind to the consistency of coffee. Place them on a plate. Beat the egg in a bowl and place the flour on a plate. Dip the lamb very lightly in the flour, shaking off the excess, then dip it in the egg, then into the mushrooms. Pat the mushrooms to adhere; you want to coat the lamb heavily. Refrigerate for up to 2 hours, if time allows. Preheat the oven to 250°C/475°F/gas 9.

3 Heat half the olive oil in a 25-cm/10-in frying pan and add the shiitake mushrooms, garlic and thyme. Cook, stirring occasionally, until the mushrooms are tender, about 10 minutes.

4 Meanwhile, place the remaining oil in an ovenproof frying pan and turn the heat to medium-high. A minute later, add the lamb; cook for 2 minutes on one side, then turn over the lamb and place the pan in the oven for 3 to 4 minutes for rare meat, a little longer if you like it better done.

5 Leave the lamb to rest for a minute, then cut it into 2-cm/½-in-thick slices. Place a dollop of leek purée on each plate, top with a portion of mushrooms, then place the lamb on top. Sprinkle with a little sea salt and serve.

You can use this spice rub with any cut of lamb (or beef, for that matter; it's great on grilled steak), but small racks are easy and festive. And the crispy chops are sensational set off against the cool relish.

Pierre Schutz, the Vong chef who developed this recipe, serves it with Peppery Green Beans (page 127), blanched green beans, or steamed spinach.

SERVES 4

9-SPICE RACK OF LAMB WITH CUCUMBER RELISH

1 teaspoon cardamom pods or ½ teaspoon ground cardamom

1 teaspoon sesame seeds

1 teaspoon fenugreek seeds or ground fenugreek

2.5-cm/1-in piece cinnamon stick

1 clove

1 teaspoon cumin seeds or powdered cumin

½ teaspoon dried red pepper flakes

½ nutmeg, smashed into a couple of chunks with the side of a cleaver

1 teaspoon ground mace

1 cucumber

Salt

12 to 15 mint leaves

Four 3-rib racks of lamb (2 racks, each cut in half)

Freshly ground black pepper

1 tablespoon peanut or other oil

1 Preheat the oven to 250°C/475°F/gas 9. Combine the spices in a dry frying pan and toast over medium-high heat, shaking the pan frequently, until the mixture starts to smoke and becomes aromatic, about 2 minutes. Grind the spices together in a coffee or spice grinder; stop before the mixture becomes powdery – it should have the texture of coarsely ground, even cracked, black pepper. (You can store this mixture in an opaque covered container for up to a year.)

2 Peel the cucumber, cut in half, and scoop out the seeds with a spoon. Cut into 2–3-cm/½–1-in sections – the size is not critical. Sprinkle with salt and toss with the mint. Transfer to a food processor and blend, stopping the machine to scrape down the mixture once or twice, until finely minced but not puréed. Place in a strainer but don't press to remove all the liquid; it should remain moist.

3 Cut little 'x's in the fat of the racks; this allows them to become extra crisp. Season with salt and pepper, then sprinkle all over with the spice mixture.

4 Heat a large ovenproof frying pan over high heat for about 2 minutes. Add the peanut oil, swirl it around the pan and pour it out so that only a film of oil remains. Brown the lamb on the meaty side for 2 minutes, then on the bony side for 1 minute. Turn the lamb on its meaty side again and place the pan in the oven. Roast for 8 minutes for very rare, 10 minutes for rare, 12 minutes for medium-rare to medium. Serve the racks with a scoop of the cucumber relish on the side.

The lovely golden colour of the sauce gracing these lamb chops is far from the colour you get using a traditional meat sauce, which is why Jean-Georges likes it so much – in fact, it's a chicken broth strongly flavoured with vegetables and fortified with horseradish. 'The contrast between sauce and meat is great,' he says. Use as much horseradish as you like; the sauce should be very assertive.

You don't need an accompaniment, but this is a nice dish to precede with soup. Try Mushroom Soup with Greens (page 27) or Parsley Soup with Mixed Mushrooms (page 28).

SERVES 4

LAMB CHOPS WITH ROOT VEGETABLES AND HORSERADISH

8 spring onions, trimmed, or 4 baby onions, peeled

4 to 6 small turnips, trimmed and peeled

2 small leeks, white part only, well washed

4 celery stalks, trimmed

3 medium carrots

25g/1oz butter

Salt

470ml/16fl oz Rich Chicken Stock (page 195) or other stock

4 large or 8 small lamb chops

Freshly ground black pepper

2 tablespoons extra virgin olive oil

1 You can cut the vegetables by hand, on a mandoline, or with the shredding disk of a food processor; in any case, you want the pieces small and thin. Preheat the oven to 250°C/475°F/gas 9.

2 Place the butter in a large frying pan over medium-high heat. When it starts to melt, add the vegetables, a couple of pinches of salt and 2 tablespoons of water. Stir once and cover. Cook, stirring occasionally, until the vegetables are limp but retain a bit of crunch, for about 7 minutes. Remove with a slotted spoon.

3 Add the stock to the pan and reduce over high heat by about one-third. This will take about 10 minutes. Then reduce the heat to low.

4 Sprinkle the lamb chops with salt and pepper. Place the olive oil in a large ovenproof frying pan and turn the heat to high. Add the chops, along with the garlic and thyme, and cook for about 2 minutes, or until nicely browned on one side. Turn over the chops and place the frying pan in the oven; roast for 4 to 8 minutes depending on the thickness of the chops and the degree of doneness you like.

2 garlic cloves, lightly crushed

4 thyme sprigs

2 tablespoons freshly grated or prepared horseradish, or more to taste

Cayenne pepper

2 tablespoons lemon juice

5 While the chops are cooking, stir the horseradish, salt and cayenne to taste, and lemon juice into the stock, together with the cooked vegetables. Taste and adjust the seasoning.

6 To serve, place 1 or 2 lamb chops on each plate and top with the sauce and vegetables.

Despite the large number of ingredients, this recipe – which Jean-Georges credits to Keith Williams, one of the talented and hardworking sous-chefs at Vong – is so well balanced you can taste every one in the sauce. Keith likes to make this dish with baby back ribs, but you can use any ribs you like. Since it's all done in the oven, this is an easy recipe to multiply for a crowd, too.

Serve with Sticky Rice Steamed in Banana Leaves (page 145) and a refreshing salad, perhaps simple greens dressed with Ginger Vinaigrette (page 210).

SERVES 4 AS A MAIN-COURSE
OR 8 FOR APPETISERS

PEANUT-CRUSTED RIBS

2 racks baby back ribs of pork, each weighing about 1kg/2lb

125ml/4fl oz white vinegar

150ml/5fl oz soy sauce

1 knob of ginger, about 10cm/4in, roughly chopped

15g/½oz butter

1 small red onion, minced

1 garlic clove, minced

1 tablespoon palm or brown sugar

2 tablespoons tomato ketchup

3 plum tomatoes, coarsely chopped (canned are fine; drain them first)

1 tablespoon Dijon mustard

1 tablespoon honey

½ teaspoon cayenne pepper

2 teaspoons chilli powder

2 teaspoons paprika pepper

1 Place the ribs in a saucepan with the white vinegar and water to cover; turn the heat to high and bring to the boil. Reduce the heat so that the liquid simmers and cook for 40 minutes. Prepare the ingredients for the sauce, and start it if you like.

2 Preheat the oven to 180°C/350°F/gas 4. Drain and cool the ribs, then peel off any membrane from their back sides.

3 Combine the 125ml/4fl oz of soy sauce with the same amount of water and the ginger in the bottom of a roasting pan. Put the ribs in the pan, meaty side up, and put the pan in the oven. Set a timer for 1 hour and 45 minutes. (If you've made the sauce already, don't begin to baste the ribs for about 30 minutes. If you haven't made the sauce, start now.)

4 To make the sauce, place the butter in a frying pan and turn the heat to medium-high. Add the onion and garlic; cook, stirring, until softened, for 5 to 10 minutes. Add the sugar and stir, then add the ketchup, tomatoes, mustard, honey, cayenne, chilli powder, paprika and Worcestershire sauce. Adjust the heat so that the mixture just simmers; cook, stirring occasionally, for 20 minutes, or until thick.

5 Stir in the chilli paste, peanut butter, reserved 2 tablespoons of soy, and the tamarind. Return to a simmer and begin basting the ribs. Baste every 10 minutes or so. Turn over the ribs about halfway through the cooking time, cook bone side up for 15 minutes, and turn over again. After 1 hour and 45

2 teaspoons Worcestershire sauce

1 tablespoon Vong Chilli Paste
(page 215), or use chilli-garlic paste
(available in Asian markets)

2 tablespoons peanut butter

2 tablespoons tamarind purée
(available at Asian markets or see
Note)

50g/2oz shelled roasted peanuts,
minced

minutes total cooking time, the ribs should be nearly falling from the bone – that's how you want them.

6 When the ribs are done, you can set them aside for up to 24 hours – cool, then wrap the whole pan (including the soy juice on the bottom) and refrigerate. To finish the ribs, brush them one more time with the sauce, then sprinkle them with the peanuts. Reheat at 180°C/350°F/gas 4 for 5 minutes (if you have just removed them from the oven) to 20 minutes (if they were refrigerated). Serve hot.

NOTE:

To make tamarind purée, place 500g/1lb tamarind pulp (available at Asian markets) in a saucepan with 250ml/9fl oz water and turn the heat to medium. Cook, whisking lightly to break up the lumps, and add more water whenever the mixture becomes dry, until you've added a total of about 470ml/16fl oz. The process will take about 10 minutes; the result will be quite thick, but fairly smooth. Put the tamarind through a food mill; you will have about 250ml/9fl oz of purée.

The sweet-and-salty caramel sauce is classic Vietnamese, but Jean-Georges's addition of shallots, and especially butter, makes this unique.

A simple winner; serve with Sticky Rice Steamed in Banana Leaves (page 145).

SERVES 4

PORK IN CARAMEL SAUCE

75g/2½oz sugar

4 tablespoons nam pla or nuoc mam (Asian fish sauce)

4 shallots, thinly sliced (use a mandoline if you have one)

1 teaspoon freshly ground black pepper

1 tablespoon sherry vinegar

500g/1lb pork or veal loin or tenderloin, cut into 4 equal pieces

Salt

1 tablespoon vegetable, grapeseed or other neutral-flavoured oil

15g/½oz butter

Coarse sea salt (optional)

1 Place the sugar in a small, heavy saucepan over medium-high heat. Cook, shaking the pan occasionally, until it melts and turns the same colour as nam pla – dark golden brown. Remove from the heat and, at arm's length (this will spatter), add the nam pla.

2 Return the pan to the stove, turn the heat to low, and add the shallots; cook, stirring, for about 5 minutes, until the shallots are tender and the sauce is a gorgeous shade of brown. Add the black pepper and set aside to cool.

3 Add the vinegar to the sauce and stir. Season the meat very lightly with salt, then place it on a plate with about ⅔ of the sauce.

4 Place the oil in a large frying pan and turn the heat to high. When it smokes, add the meat and cook on one side until it browns, for about 2 minutes. Turn over the meat and cook it on the other side for 1 minute.

5 Reduce the heat to medium and add the butter, together with half of the sauce from the plate (discard the remaining sauce on the plate). Cook, turning as necessary, until the meat is beautifully browned on both sides. Dress with the reserved sauce, sprinkle with a little sea salt, if you like, and serve.

Baeckoffe is Alsatian for baker's oven. On Sunday morning, housewives would prepare this simple stew and drop it off at the baker's before church. By lunchtime, it was done. This is truly unattended cooking.

Feel free to substitute lamb or beef for the pork. And feel free, too, to make this a day in advance; like many stews, it is better the second day.

BAECKOFFE OF PORK

750g/1½lb potatoes, peeled and sliced thin

500g/1lb boneless pork, preferably from the shoulder

1 medium carrot, cut into chunks

1 leek, trimmed of hard green parts, cut in half, and well washed

1 medium onion, chopped

1 tablespoon chopped garlic

50g/2oz roughly chopped parsley

Salt and freshly ground black pepper

3 thick slices tomato

250ml/9fl oz dry white wine, preferably Riesling or Pinot Blanc

Mustard

Coarse sea salt

1 Rinse the potatoes in several changes of water to remove all traces of starch. Remove the excess fat from the meat and cut it into 3–4-cm/1–1½-in chunks. Preheat the oven to 160°C/325°F/gas 3.

2 In a 2–2.5-l/3–4-pint covered casserole (no larger), layer about one-third of the potatoes, followed by a bit less than half the carrot, leek, onion, garlic, parsley, salt and plenty of pepper. Add half the meat and some more salt and pepper. Repeat, finishing with a layer of potato and a sprinkling of the remaining vegetables. Top with the tomato and pour in the wine.

3 Cover and bake for 2 to 3 hours, or until the top is crusted. Leave to rest for a few minutes, then serve, passing around the mustard and sea salt at the table.

VEGETABLES

This quick, simple and lovely dish can be given four-star elegance if you choose to make the optional asparagus *jus* (see below). It makes great use of peelings and trimmings and, as Jean-Georges says, 'I think the peelings actually have more flavour than the interior.' Do not use pencil-thin asparagus here; in fact, the thicker the better.

These make a nice first course, or a good side dish for something straightforward like Roast Poussins with Herb-Bread Stuffing (page 96).

SERVES 2 AS A MAIN-COURSE OR
4 AS AN APPETISER

ASPARAGUS WITH MIXED MUSHROOMS AND PARMESAN

About 500g/1lb of the largest asparagus you can find (12 jumbo)

4 tablespoons extra virgin olive oil

375g/¾lb mixed mushrooms, trimmed, washed, and roughly chopped

1 shallot, minced

2 garlic cloves, minced

Salt and freshly ground black pepper

50g/2oz freshly grated Parmesan cheese

25g/1oz chopped chives

1 Put a large pot of salted water on to boil. Make the asparagus *jus* if you like (next page).

2 Place 2 tablespoons of olive oil in a 25-cm/10-in frying pan and turn the heat to medium-high. Add the mushrooms, shallot and garlic, along with a sprinkling of salt and pepper. Cook over medium heat, stirring occasionally, until most of the mushroom liquid evaporates, in about 10 minutes. Turn off the heat, but keep the mushrooms warm.

3 Meanwhile, poach the asparagus spears in the boiling water, just until they begin to become tender, for 2 to 4 minutes depending on their thickness. They should still be slightly crunchy. Plunge them into iced water, drain, then dry on kitchen roll.

4 Place the remaining 2 tablespoons of oil in a 30-cm/12-in frying pan and turn the heat to medium-high. When the oil is hot, add the asparagus spears. Brown them lightly, turning as each side browns. Sprinkle them with pepper, but not salt.

5 When the asparagus are lightly browned, sprinkle them with the Parmesan and shake the pan once or twice to distribute it. Stir the chives into the mushrooms.

6 To serve, place a portion of the asparagus on each plate, then top with a portion of the mushrooms. Spoon a bit of the asparagus *jus* around the plate if you like.

TO MAKE ASPARAGUS JUS

1 Reserve all the asparagus trimmings; chop the bottoms into 2-cm/½-in pieces and cook them, along with the peels, in boiling salted water to cover (use this same water to poach the asparagus afterwards). When very tender, after 6 to 10 minutes, drain, reserving about 4 tablespoons of the cooking liquid. Purée the trimmings in a blender, adding as much of the reserved cooking liquid as necessary.

2 Heat 1 tablespoon of butter in a small saucepan over medium heat. When it melts, add the purée, salt and pepper. Heat through, taste and adjust seasoning, and keep warm until ready to serve.

There is no faster way to cook artichokes than this, and the flavour combination is surprising (and especially delicious if you use All-Purpose Curry Powder, page 214). If you use baby artichokes, you won't have to remove the choke.

These artichokes are perfect alongside Oven-Crisped Chicken with Fragrant Spices (page 92), or even simple roast chicken or steamed fish.

SERVES 4

CURRIED ARTICHOKES

4 to 6 baby artichokes

2 tablespoons butter or peanut oil

Salt

About 1 teaspoon All-Purpose Curry Powder (page 214) or commercial curry powder

1 Cut off the bottom stem and top spikes from the artichokes. Then cut all around the outside of the artichokes, removing and discarding all the hard leaves. Slice the artichokes as thinly as possible with a knife or, better still, a mandoline.

2 Place the butter or oil in a 25-cm/10-in frying pan and turn the heat to medium-high. Sprinkle the artichokes with salt and curry powder. When the butter foam subsides or the oil is hot, toss in the artichokes. Cook, shaking the pan a little bit from time to time, for 3 minutes.

3 Add 4 tablespoons of water to the pan and continue to cook, shaking the pan now and then. When the water evaporates, after 5 or 10 minutes, the artichokes are done. Serve hot or at room temperature.

Jean-Georges serves these with Chicken with Lemongrass (page 90), but they're a great accompaniment for any main course that can stand up to the assertive combination of soy and black pepper, such as 9-Spice Rack of Lamb (page 115).

SERVES 4

PEPPERY GREEN BEANS

1 tablespoon vegetable, grapeseed or other neutral-flavoured oil

50g/2oz peeled, deseeded and minced red capsicum pepper

1 medium onion, sliced

500g/1lb green beans, trimmed and cut into 8–10-cm/3–4-in lengths

4 tablespoons soy sauce

½ teaspoon freshly crushed black peppercorns, or more to taste

1 Place the oil in a large frying pan and turn the heat to medium. Add the red pepper and onion and cook, stirring occasionally, until the onion is soft, for 3 to 5 minutes. Reduce the heat to medium-low and cook until the onion is very tender, for another 5 minutes or so.

2 Add the beans and return the heat to high; cook for 1 minute. Add the soy sauce and 125ml/4fl oz of water. Cook at a lively boil for a few minutes, until most of the liquid has evaporated and the beans are green and crisp-tender. (Add a little more water if necessary.)

3 Add the black pepper and continue to cook until there are only about 2 tablespoons of liquid left in the pan. Taste and adjust seasoning, then serve hot or at room temperature.

A *very* simple preparation that accentuates the sweet nature of these root vegetables. Use small beetroots and turnips, if possible, or cut larger ones into chunks. If you remove the pan when a tablespoon or two of beetroot juice remains in the bottom you can use it as a sauce with which to decorate a plate. Serve with Duck à la JoJo (page 100) or other full-flavoured meat dishes.

SERVES 4

Use this technique with beetroots or turnips alone, or with any other root vegetable, such as carrots, parsnips or potatoes.

CARAMELISED BEETROOTS AND TURNIPS

250–300g/8–10oz beetroots, preferably less than 5cm/2in in diameter

250–300g/8–10oz turnips, preferably less than 5cm/2in in diameter

Salt

25g/1oz butter

1 Peel and trim the beetroots and turnips; quarter them if they are large. Place each in its own saucepan with a pinch of salt and water to come about halfway up their height. Divide the butter between the two pans, cover each, and turn the heat to medium-high.

2 Simmer until the vegetables are nearly tender, about 20 minutes. Uncover; much of the water will have evaporated. Continue to cook until the vegetables are shiny and glazed with their juices. Add more salt, if necessary, and serve hot.

The combination of flavoured bread crumbs and yogurt makes this fun sauce a good dip for almost any vegetable, and also for hot or cold sautéed chicken.

Although Jean-Georges usually plunges blanched vegetables into iced water to stop their cooking, he doesn't use that technique for broccoli: 'it leaches out too much flavour,' he says. Remove the broccoli from the boiling water when it is just barely tender; it will retain enough heat to continue to cook for a couple of minutes.

SERVES 4

DIP 'N' EAT BROCCOLI

500g/1lb broccoli tops, separated into florets

Salt

3 tablespoons vegetable, grapeseed or other neutral-flavoured oil

40g/1½oz fresh, coarse breadcrumbs

1 teaspoon ground cardamom (preferably freshly ground from seeds)

250ml/9fl oz plain yogurt (low-fat or nonfat is fine)

1 To steam the broccoli, place it in a basket or on a rack over boiling water and cover. Cook the broccoli until it is bright green and just tender, for about 7 minutes. To boil, place the broccoli in boiling salted water and cook until it is bright green and just tender, for about 7 minutes. Remove and drain immediately.

2 Meanwhile, place the oil in a 25-cm/10-in frying pan over medium heat. A minute later, add the breadcrumbs and increase the heat to high. Cook, stirring or shaking the pan until the crumbs brown, just a little over a minute. (Alternatively, bake the crumbs on a baking tray with no oil in a preheated 180°C/350°F/gas 4 oven until brown, tossing occasionally, about 15 minutes.) Drain the crumbs quickly in a strainer or colander, then use kitchen roll to remove as much of the remaining oil as possible.

3 Combine the breadcrumbs, cardamom and 1 teaspoon of salt.

4 To serve, place a portion of broccoli on each plate with a spoonful of yogurt and a portion of the breadcrumbs. To eat, dip the broccoli into the yogurt, then into the breadcrumbs.

This slow-cooking technique (Jean-Georges calls the result a *confit*) intensifies the flavour of the carrots. And you can make this dish days in advance; just refrigerate, then reheat – even in a microwave. Add the lemon juice and coriander at the last minute.

SERVES 4

Jean-Georges serves this almost as a sauce with unsauced steamed fish or with Sautéed Chicken with Green Olives and Coriander (page 89).

SIMMERED CARROTS WITH CUMIN AND ORANGE

500g/1lb carrots, the fresher the better, preferably about 2cm/3/4in at their thickest part and 15–20cm/6–8in long

1 teaspoon cumin seeds (*not* ground cumin)

1 teaspoon grated or minced orange zest

1 teaspoon minced garlic

4 tablespoons extra virgin olive oil

Pinch of salt

$^1/_8$ teaspoon sugar

250ml/9fl oz orange juice, preferably freshly squeezed

1 teaspoon lime or lemon juice

2 tablespoons chopped coriander

1 Trim and peel the carrots; leave them whole if they are the size recommended above (if your carrots are bigger, peel them and cut them into chunks or in half the long way). Select a saucepan large enough to hold them, and place the cumin, orange zest, garlic, oil, salt, sugar and orange juice in it. Turn the heat to medium and bring to the boil, stirring.

2 Add the carrots, cover, and turn the heat to low. The mixture should be bubbling gently, not vigorously, whenever you remove the cover. Cook, virtually undisturbed (you can check the progress if you like) for about 1$^1/_2$ hours, or until the carrots are very tender but not yet falling apart.

3 Gently stir the lime juice into the carrots. Sprinkle with coriander, stir once, and serve.

APPLE CONFIT, SABLEUSE, GREEN APPLE SORBET

WARM, SOFT CHOCOLATE CAKE

WITH CARAMEL ICE CREAM

LACQUERED PEACH

BONELESS LAMB WITH

MUSHROOM CRUST AND LEEK PUREE

COUNTER-CLOCKWISE: SHRIMP SATAY,

MARINATED QUAIL, SEARED TUNA ROLL,

RICE PAPER ROLLS, CRAB SPRING ROLLS,

WITH FOUR DIPPING SAUCES

SALMON AND POTATO CRISPS

WITH HORSERADISH CREAM

FROM TOP TO BOTTOM: FRESH PEA SOUP,

CREAMY BUTTERNUT SQUASH SOUP, CHICKEN SOUP

WITH COCONUT MILK AND LEMONGRASS

BEEF WITH GINGER

Like any corn relish, this one – developed by Vong chef Pierre Schutz – nicely complements grilled meat, Chicken with Lemongrass (page 90), or Oven-Crisped Chicken with Fragrant Spices (page 92).

There is enough mincing to do here to keep you busy for a few minutes, but if you're careful you can use the food processor and reduce the work to 30 seconds: combine the onion and pepper and pulse briefly, scraping down the sides between pulses. Do not over-process.

Note the interesting possibility of making corn-cob stock to use as the liquid here.

SERVES 4

SPICY STIR-FRIED CORN

4 fresh ears corn

2 tablespoons vegetable, grapeseed or other neutral-flavoured oil

1 stalk lemongrass, trimmed to reveal the tender inner core, then minced to give 2 tablespoons

2 teaspoons minced garlic

1 tablespoon butter

1 medium onion, minced

250ml/9fl oz Rich Chicken Stock (page 195) or any chicken stock, (optional)

2 teaspoons minced lime leaves or lime zest

2 tablespoons nam pla or nuoc mam (Asian fish sauce)

1 teaspoon Vong Chilli Paste (page 215), or cayenne pepper to taste

2 tablespoons lime juice

Minced coriander

1 Strip the kernels from the corn. If you don't have chicken stock, or prefer not to use it, cut up the cobs and steam them in a covered saucepan with 300ml/½ pint of water for about 10 minutes, then strain and measure 250ml/9fl oz.

2 Place the oil in a large frying pan and turn the heat to high. Add the lemongrass; when it starts to brown, add the garlic, then the butter, the onion and finally the corn. Keep the heat high and let the mixture brown, even if some of it sticks to the bottom of the frying pan.

3 When most of the corn kernels have browned, add the corn or chicken stock and cook for 2 minutes, stirring and scraping. Add the lime leaves or zest, nam pla, chilli paste or cayenne and lime juice. Stir and cook for 30 seconds more, then turn off the heat. Garnish with the coriander and serve immediately.

This simple dish is a natural choice to serve with any meat that features Asian seasonings, such as Peanut-

Crusted Ribs (page 118).

SERVES 4

GRILLED AUBERGINE WITH NAM PLA AND BASIL

4 to 8 small-to-medium aubergines, preferably a variety of colours, about 750g/1½lb total, rinsed

Juice of 1 lemon

About 1 tablespoon nam pla or nuoc mam (Asian fish sauce)

A few leaves Thai or other basil

1 Start a charcoal or wood fire in a grill or preheat a gas grill; the fire should be quite hot.

2 Grill the aubergines whole, turning occasionally, until the skin is charred and the aubergines collapse, in about 20 minutes. Remove from the heat and remove the skins with a paring knife. As you're doing so, the aubergines will fall apart; that's fine.

3 Sprinkle each aubergine with some lemon juice and fish sauce. Garnish with basil leaves, whole if they're small, torn if they're larger. Serve hot or at room temperature.

Serve these as a side dish, float them on top of soup, or lay them under smoked salmon and a dollop of sour cream. They have never got that far when I've made them, with or without Jean-Georges, because they are best straight from the frying pan.

Fresh peas, obviously, are ideal but frozen peas are a good substitute.

 # FRESH PEA PANCAKE

250g/½lb fresh or frozen and thawed shelled peas

1 egg

1 tablespoon flour

Salt and freshly ground black pepper

About 2 tablespoons vegetable, grapeseed or other neutral-flavoured oil

1 Bring a small pot of water to the boil and blanch the peas for 1 minute. Drain, then run under cold water until cold.

2 Set 50g/2oz of peas aside and purée the remaining peas in a blender with the egg and 2 tablespoons of water until smooth.

3 Place the purée in a bowl and beat in the flour, along with a pinch of salt, pepper, and the reserved whole peas.

4 Place 1 tablespoon of oil in a large frying pan and turn the heat to medium. When the oil is hot, pour most of it out; you just need enough to film the bottom of the pan.

5 Spoon the batter into the frying pan using a tablespoon, making pancakes about 5cm/2in across. Cook gently for about 3 minutes per side, taking care to cook them through before they brown too much. Add more oil as necessary and continue to cook until all the batter is used up. These are best hot, but not at all bad at room temperature.

A sweet-and-spicy, easy-to-make condiment that complements any roasted meat or chicken beautifully, but is especially well suited to Duck à la JoJo (page 100).

SHALLOT CONFIT WITH HONEY AND GINGER

4 tablespoons peeled and finely minced ginger

175g/6oz sliced shallots

250g/9oz honey

190ml/6fl oz red wine vinegar

1 Place the ginger, shallots and honey in a saucepan and turn the heat to medium. Cook, stirring only occasionally, for about 15 minutes, or until the shallots have given up their liquid and the mixture is lightly browned and almost dry.

2 Stir in the vinegar and, with the heat still at medium, reduce by about half; this will take 5 to 10 minutes.

3 When the mixture is syrupy, add 190ml/6fl oz of water and cook for another 5 to 10 minutes, until the mixture is moist and syrupy (not soupy) and very deep golden. Serve hot or at room temperature. This keeps well, covered and refrigerated, for up to a week; warm or bring to room temperature before serving.

Guaranteed to produce the sweetest oven-dried tomatoes you've ever tasted (eat the garlic, too). Fresh thyme, though not absolutely essential, adds a beguiling fragrance you won't get with dried thyme.

Double the recipe if your oven is big enough, and save some for

SERVES 4 – 6   Red Snapper with Tomato Confit and Tapenade (page 82).

TOMATO CONFIT

12 plum tomatoes, ripe but not too soft

6 tablespoons extra virgin olive oil

6 garlic cloves, lightly crushed

6 thyme sprigs

1 teaspoon coarse sea salt

1 Cut out the hard stem end of each of the tomatoes and make an 'x' in the flower end. Plunge into boiling water for about 15 seconds, or until the skins loosen. Plunge into iced water and drain. Peel, cut in half, and use your fingers to dig out the seeds. Preheat the oven to 140°C/275°F/gas 1.

2 Cover a baking sheet with aluminum foil and brush it with the olive oil. Place the tomatoes on the oil, cut side down. Scatter the garlic and thyme around, and sprinkle with the salt and remaining olive oil.

3 Bake for 2 hours or more, checking every half hour or so to make sure that the tomatoes are not browning (if they are, reduce the heat) and turning the baking sheet so the tomatoes cook evenly. The tomatoes are done when they are very soft and shrivelled.

Not exactly a jam, but not far from it. Jean-Georges serves this chutney with Poached Fish with Fennel (page 76), but it's also beautiful with Braised Duck and Vegetables with Asian Spices (page 102) and 9-Spice Rack of Lamb (page 115).

Don't try to cook this without the overnight resting period, which draws the juices from the tomatoes, giving them a flavourful liquid in which to simmer.

MAKES ABOUT 375ML/13FL OZ

GREEN TOMATO MARMALADE

500g/1lb green tomatoes, cored and roughly chopped

125g/4oz sugar

Juice of 1 lemon

1 Combine all ingredients, cover and refrigerate overnight.

2 Place in a heavy saucepan over medium-high heat and bring to a boil. Adjust the heat so the mixture is simmering steadily, but not boiling furiously.

3 Cook, stirring occasionally to prevent burning, for at least 2 hours, until the tomatoes are tender and sweet. Cool and refrigerate in a covered container; this will keep for at least a week. Bring to room temperature before serving.

The perfect side dish for a Harvest Festival dinner, and equally good when reheated. For the sake of elegance, Jean-Georges removes the bacon before serving; but when we made it together, we sliced the bacon and ate it on slices of bread.

Serve this, if you like, with Grilled Chicken Breast with Cloves (page 93).

MAKES 4 MAIN-COURSE OR AT LEAST 8 SIDE-DISH SERVINGS

GLAZED AUTUMN VEGETABLES AND FRUITS

8 large garlic cloves, not peeled

250g/½lb Swiss chard, red or green, stems cut into 5-cm/2-in lengths

4 tablespoons olive oil

2 medium carrots, cut into small chunks

12 radishes, cut into quarters

6 small waxy potatoes, scrubbed and cut in half

2 or 3 small turnips, peeled and cut into chunks

1 large apple, peeled, cored and cut into slices

1 large pear, peeled, cored and cut into slices

125g/4oz seedless grapes

250g/½lb back bacon, cut into chunks

250g/½lb shiitake mushrooms, stems removed and discarded or reserved for stock, caps cut into chunks

250ml/9fl oz Rich Chicken Stock (page 195) or other stock

Salt and freshly ground black pepper

1 Bring a large pot of water to the boil. Blanch the garlic for 1 minute, then remove with a slotted spoon. Rinse in cold water and drain. Peel, leave whole.

2 Blanch the chard leaves in the same water for 1 minute; remove to a bowl of iced water, drain and slice into thin shreds.

3 Heat 2 tablespoons of olive oil over medium heat in a large frying pan. Add the chard stems, carrots, radishes, potatoes and turnips and cook over high heat, stirring, for 5 to 10 minutes, until browned. Remove and set aside.

4 Cook the fruit in the same pan, stirring, for about 5 minutes. Remove and set aside.

5 Place the remaining olive oil in a large, heavy saucepan with the bacon and turn the heat to medium-high. Add the garlic and shiitakes and cook until the bacon browns a little bit; then add all the vegetables except the chard leaves.

6 Cook for 2 minutes, stir, then add the stock. Reduce the heat to medium, add salt and pepper to taste, cover and reduce the heat to medium-low. Cook for 15 minutes.

7 Add the fruit, stir, replace the cover, and cook for 10 minutes, stirring once or twice.

8 Uncover; most of the liquid will have evaporated and there will be a glaze. If not, cook over medium heat for a couple of minutes more. Adjust the seasoning and stir in the chard leaves. Remove the bacon, if you like, and serve.

V
E
G
E
T
A
B
L
E
S

PASTA GRAINS AND RICE

Not only is this unusual pasta dish a fine way to use beetroot tops, it's beautiful – the filling is pink; the sauce beetroot red. If you can get a variety of white, red and golden beetroots, the dish will look even better.

If you serve this as a first course, as Jean-Georges does, follow it with something light but flavourful, such as Scallops and Cauliflower

MAKES 40 TO 50 RAVIOLI; 4 LARGE OR 8 SMALL PORTIONS with Caper-Raisin Sauce (page 60).

 # BEETROOT TOP RAVIOLI WITH BEETROOT SAUCE

500g/1lb beetroot tops

2 tablespoons olive oil

1 medium onion, minced

1 garlic clove, minced

Salt and freshly ground black pepper

125g/4oz ricotta

150g/5oz freshly grated Parmesan cheese

230g/7oz flour, plus some for dusting the work surface

7 egg yolks

1 egg

4 medium beetroots (about 500g/1lb), peeled and sliced

130g/4½oz butter

1½ tablespoons lemon juice

1 tablespoon minced fresh sage leaves

1 Wash the beetroot tops in several changes of water. Trim and discard the thick ends of the stems. Cook the leaves in boiling salted water to cover for about 5 minutes, or until they are very tender. Drain, rinse in cold water, then drain again. Squeeze out the liquid and chop the leaves.

2 Place the olive oil in a medium frying pan and turn the heat to medium-high. Add the onion, garlic and a pinch of salt. Cook, stirring, for about 10 minutes, until very tender but not brown.

3 Cool the onion mixture slightly, then combine with the leaves, ricotta, Parmesan and black pepper. Cover and refrigerate for at least 1 hour or overnight.

4 Combine the flour, 5 egg yolks and the whole egg in a bowl and mix well. If the dough does not come together after a minute or so, add a tablespoon or more of water. Knead until smooth, for about 2 minutes, then wrap in clingfilm and refrigerate for at least 1 hour or overnight.

5 Divide the dough in half and sprinkle each half with some flour. Put it through a pasta machine (or use a rolling pin), making the dough progressively thinner, and dusting with flour between rolls. The dough is ready when it is so thin you can see your hand through it. Place it on a large work surface and use a pastry cutter to make 8cm/3in rounds. Combine the scraps from the first batch with the second portion of dough and repeat.

6 Beat the remaining egg yolks and brush each of the rounds with yolk. Place a rounded teaspoon of the filling on each; fold and crimp to seal. Place each ravioli on a floured board when you are finished. Bring a large pot of salted water to the boil.

7 Combine the beetroots with 1 tablespoon of butter and water to cover in a small saucepan; add a pinch of salt. Cover and turn the heat to high, then cook for 20 to 30 minutes, until only 3 tablespoons of liquid remain.

8 When the beetroots are ready, cook the ravioli in several batches in the boiling water; they will be done in about 2 minutes. Remove them with a slotted spoon and keep them warm by placing them in a bowl in a low oven.

9 Finally, melt the remaining butter in a saucepan over medium heat; let it brown a bit, then add the lemon juice, beetroot cooking liquid, and sage. Serve the ravioli with a little of this sauce drizzled over, and a few beetroot slices on the side.

Almost a corn pudding, this is sweet, creamy and crisp. It can also be made all-year-round, because Jean-Georges, with no apologies, uses canned corn here. 'I don't know why, but this doesn't work as well with fresh corn. The flavour of canned corn comes out better when you mix it with the other ingredients,' he says.

This amount of batter makes a 20–25-cm/8–10-in pancake or four 8–10-cm/3–4-in pancakes. For the latter, you'll need four small pans and four free burners; divide the oil among the pans and reduce the baking time by about one-third. You can serve it with almost anything.

SERVES 4 – 6

CORN CAKE

225g/7oz drained canned corn

250ml/9fl oz cream

2 tablespoons milk

50g/2oz flour

1 egg

1 egg yolk

Salt and freshly ground black pepper

¼ teaspoon freshly grated nutmeg

2½ tablespoons vegetable, grapeseed or other neutral-flavoured oil

1 tablespoon butter

1 Preheat the oven to 250°C/475°F/gas 9. Combine 150g/5oz corn with the cream, milk, flour, egg and egg yolk in a food processor. Process until smooth, for about 1 minute, stopping the machine and scraping down the container's sides if necessary.

2 By hand, stir in the remaining corn, a pinch of salt, lots of freshly ground black pepper and the nutmeg.

3 Heat an 20–25-cm/8–10-in ovenproof frying pan, preferably nonstick, over high heat for a couple of minutes. Add the oil and, when the oil begins to smoke, the batter. Cook over high heat, for 2 or 3 minutes, until the edges firm up and a few bubbles appear on surface, then transfer the pan to the oven. Bake for about 5 minutes, then turn it over carefully. (You can do this with a spatula, or slide the cake out onto a plate, place another plate over it, invert the 2 plates, and slide the cake back into the pan.) Return it to the top of the stove over medium-high heat.

4 Break the butter into a few pieces and place them around the edge of the cake. Cook over medium heat, for 3 minutes or so, until the bottom is nicely browned. Sprinkle with salt and serve.

In an article about grains, I had just finished writing something like 'I know of no way of cooking millet that's worth the effort,' when Jean-Georges served me this wonderful cake. It turns out Jean-Georges's chef de cuisine Didier Virot felt the same way as I and decided to do something about it. Millet is a small round grain and can be found in supermarkets or health food stores.

SERVES 4

Like Corn Cake (page 142), Millet Cake can be served with almost anything, but especially with stews.

MILLET CAKE

200g/7oz millet

Salt

50g/2oz butter, melted

2 eggs

2 yolks

4 tabelspoons milk

Freshly ground black pepper

1 tablespoon vegetable, grapeseed or other neutral-flavoured oil

1 Preheat the oven to 250°C/475°F/gas 9. Combine the millet, 470ml/16fl oz of water, and a pinch of salt in a saucepan, cover, and place over medium-high heat for about 20 minutes, or until the water is absorbed. Turn off the heat and leave it to sit, covered, for 10 more minutes.

2 Stir in the butter, whole eggs, egg yolks, milk and salt and pepper to taste.

3 Place an 20–25-cm/8–10-in ovenproof frying pan, preferably nonstick, over high heat; a minute later, add the oil. When the oil smokes, pour in the batter and cook for about 3 minutes, or until the edges firm up a bit and some bubbles appear in the middle. Transfer the pan to the oven and bake until firm on top, for about 10 minutes. To serve, invert onto a plate so the crisp side is upwards.

Jean-Georges serves pan-fried noodles with Chicken with Lemongrass (page 90), with Poussins with Onion Compôte (page 98), and with other poultry dishes.

Kids love this cake, as long as you keep the chilli paste to a minimum.

SERVES 4 – 6

PAN-FRIED NOODLE CAKE

375g/¾lb fresh egg noodles

15g/½oz minced chives

2 tablespoons Vong Chilli Paste (page 215) or chilli-garlic paste

2½ tablespoons vegetable, grapeseed or other neutral-flavoured oil

Salt

1 Put a large pot of salted water on to boil. Add the noodles and cook for 2 or 3 minutes. Do not let them get too soft, because they will cook further; they should just lose their raw flavour. Drain, rinse in cold water, then drain well.

2 Toss the noodles with the chives, chilli paste, 1 tablespoon of oil and salt; taste and adjust the seasoning as necessary. Jean-Georges makes this pancake fairly fiery, but you need not.

3 Film the bottom of a heavy 25-cm/10-in frying pan, preferably nonstick, with most of the remaining oil and turn the heat to medium-high. When the oil shimmers, add the noodle mix. Spread it out evenly and press it down a little with your hands or the back of a spatula.

4 Cook for about 2 minutes, then reduce the heat a bit and continue to cook until the cake is holding together and is nicely browned on the bottom. Flip the noodle cake, adding a little more oil if necessary. (The easiest way to do this: slide the cake out onto a plate, cover with another plate, invert the plates, and slide the cake back into the pan.)

5 Cook on the other side until brown, then serve hot or at room temperature.

The ingredients you need for this dish will keep forever in your pantry, so shop once and make this at will (which will be often, believe me). Jean-Georges insists that the rice must be steamed in the banana leaves before serving: 'That's the only floral or herbal flavour that you give to the rice.' But when you taste the rice simply mixed with the coconut milk and nam pla you may choose to cut the recipe short at the end of Step 2, as I do when I want this rice but don't have enough time for wrapping.

This is the obvious side dish for any saucy Asian preparation, such as Pork in Caramel Sauce (page 120).

SERVES 4

STICKY RICE STEAMED IN BANANA LEAVES

200g/7oz glutinous ('sticky') rice

125ml/4fl oz canned unsweetened coconut milk

1½ teaspoons nam pla or nuoc mam (Asian fish sauce)

2 to 4 banana leaves

1 Soak the rice in water to cover for at least 1 hour and preferably overnight. Drain, then wrap loosely in cheesecloth. Place in a steamer above boiling water and cook for about 8 minutes, until sticky, soft and elastic. Unwrap and leave to cool for a minute.

2 Toss the rice with the coconut milk and nam pla; taste and add more of either if you like.

3 Cut the banana leaves so you have four 20 × 25-cm/8 × 10-in rectangles, with the grain of the leaves running the long way. Place one long end closest to your body and spoon a quarter of the rice mixture onto the middle of the leaf. Fold one long end over, then the other, and finally the two shorter ends. Seal with a toothpick or string. Repeat with the remaining leaves. (At this point, you may refrigerate these packages for up to 2 days.)

4 When you're ready to serve, steam over boiling water until hot, for about 10 minutes, or microwave for a couple of minutes to reheat.

D E S S E R T S

A maceration of strawberries and citrus that produces an intoxicating (not literally) liquid. You will want to lick the bowl.

SERVES 6 – 8

FRUIT SALAD IN STRAWBERRY WATER

3 oranges

3 lemons

3 limes

225g/7oz sugar

1.5kg/3lb strawberries, hulled and cut into quarters if small, eighths if large

Lemon juice

Any assortment of fresh fruit, trimmed, peeled, pitted and cut up as necessary

1 Use a vegetable peeler to remove the zests from the citrus. Scrape off any thick pith from the inside of the zests. Combine the zests and the sugar in a large bowl.

2 Juice the citrus and strain out the pips. Add the juice to the zest-sugar mixture and stir. Add the strawberries, cover and refrigerate overnight.

3 Strain the strawberry water; taste and add lemon juice as necessary. (You will need more lemon juice if you are serving the strawberry water over very sweet fruit, like ripe peaches; less lemon juice if you have more acidic fruit, such as raspberries.)

4 Arrange some of the macerated strawberries along with an assortment of other fruit in a bowl and pour the strawberry water over it. Serve immediately.

A quick, simple cherry concoction created by Vong pastry chef Serge Decrauzat to accompany some of his slightly sour desserts, like Lemon Yogurt Sorbet (page 177).

SERVES 4

CHERRY 'SALAD'

500g/1lb cherries, stems and stones removed and reserved

125g/4oz sugar

125g/4oz black or red currants, fresh or frozen

250ml/9fl oz port

1 Crack the cherry stones by smacking them lightly with a hammer or the bottom of a saucepan; you don't need to pulverize them, just to expose their kernels. Place them in a pot with 125ml/4fl oz water, the stems and the sugar. Bring to the boil, then cook for 2 minutes, cover and cool while proceeding with the recipe.

2 Combine the currants and port in a medium saucepan and bring to the boil over high heat. Reduce by half, stirring occasionally; this will take at least 10 minutes.

3 Strain the cherry syrup into a saucepan, pressing to extract as much liquid as possible. Strain into it the currant-port mixture, without pressing.

4 Bring to the boil, add the cherries, and turn off the heat. Cover and cool, then serve.

This is among the best no-fat desserts ever – somewhere between a soup and a salad. It begins with the unusual step of making a 'stock' from crushed cherry stones, a worthwhile and not-at-all difficult exercise, which lends a distinct bitter-almond flavour to the finished product. It ends with a gorgeous, completely irresistible mélange of summer fruit, not all of which need be red.

Use fresh sour cherries if you can get them, but don't give it a moment's thought if you cannot. The combination of berries here is just a suggestion; vary it at will, using these fruits, blackberries, or fresh currants. Serve this on its own or with any sorbet.

SERVES 4 – 6

SOUP OF RED FRUITS

250g/½lb cherries, stems and stones removed and reserved

125g/4oz sugar

300g/10oz strawberries, cored and halved (or quartered if very large)

150g/5oz blueberries

150g/5oz raspberries

3 tablespoons lemon juice

Mint leaves

1 Crack the cherry stones by smacking them lightly with a hammer or the bottom of a saucepan; you don't need to pulverize them, just to expose their kernels. Place them in a saucepan with the stems, sugar and 250ml/9fl oz water. Bring to the boil over high heat. Reduce the heat to medium and cook for 5 minutes. Remove from the heat and cool slightly.

2 Strain out the stones and stems, return the liquid to the saucepan, and add the cherries. Cook over medium heat until the cherries are quite tender, in 10 to 15 minutes. Cool, then chill, either over a bowl of iced water or in the refrigerator. (You may prepare the recipe in advance up to this point; refrigerate in a covered container for up to a day.)

3 Place the berries in a bowl and pour the cherries and their juices over them. Add the lemon juice, garnish with mint leaves, and serve immediately, or refrigerate for up to a day. The mixture will become soupier the longer it sits.

At just the time I was writing a new-things-you-can-do-with-rhubarb piece for *The New York Times*, Jean-Georges asked me if I'd ever had his rhubarb soup. I had not, and was ecstatic when we made it together – nothing could be easier to make, and it's a delicious use for this underappreciated vegetable.

SERVES 4   This is a cold soup, so allow time to chill it before serving.

RHUBARB SOUP

1kg/2lb rhubarb

225g/7oz sugar

2 vanilla pods

1 String the rhubarb, then cut roughly into 5-cm/2-in lengths.

2 Place 900ml/1½ pints water in a saucepan and add the sugar; turn the heat to medium-high. Split the vanilla pods lengthwise and scrape out the seeds; add both the seeds and pods to the pot. When the water boils, reduce the heat to medium and cook for 5 minutes, then add the rhubarb. Cook for another 5 minutes or so, until the rhubarb begins to fall apart.

3 Cool to room temperature, then cover and refrigerate for several hours or overnight.

4 When you're ready to serve, remove the vanilla pods and break up the hunks of rhubarb with a whisk. Serve cold, with slices of strawberry and mango, a scoop of any sorbet, a dollop of yogurt or sour cream, or simply unadorned.

Like Apple Confit (page 154), this dessert is wonderful accompanied by a slice of Sableuse (page 167) or pound cake.

SERVES 4

You can make this last-minute dish with any fruit, even apples or pears, but berries are best.

WARM FRUIT COMPOTE

125g/4oz sugar, more or less, depending on the sweetness of the berries

2½ tablespoons butter

300g/10oz huckleberries, currants, raspberries, blueberries, or other fruit, peeled, hulled, picked over, washed, and dried, if necessary

Crème fraîche or sour cream

1 Combine 125ml/4fl oz water with the sugar and butter in a thick-bottomed saucepan and cook over medium-high heat, shaking and stirring, until the mixture is thick and syrupy, but not browned.

2 Toss in the fruit and cook over low heat until the fruit begins to break up and release its juices, for about 2 minutes (some fruits will require the addition of a little more water).

3 Serve topped with a bit of crème fraîche or sour cream (thinned with double cream, if necessary).

When Jean-Georges wanted a fruit dessert to accompany Petit Beurre (page 164), pastry chef Eric Hubert came up with this: slightly spicy and supremely tender, these apricots are good by themselves, or with Petit Beurre, or any ice cream, or cheesecake.

SERVES ABOUT 4

PEPPERED POACHED APRICOTS

2 tablespoons sugar

¼ teaspoon white pepper

10 to 12 apricots, stoned

1 Preheat the oven to 230°C/450°F/gas 8. Cut a round of greaseproof or wax paper to fit inside a heavy-bottomed ovenproof frying pan.

2 Place the sugar in the pan and turn the heat to high. Shake the pan occasionally, for 3 to 5 minutes, until the sugar is uniformly brown. Sprinkle with the pepper, then place the apricots on their sides in one layer; squeeze them in if necessary.

3 Add 4 tablespoons of water and cover the apricots with the paper. Bake for about 15 minutes, or until extremely tender. Cool and serve.

Developed by Eric Hubert, who has worked with Jean-Georges as pastry chef for years, this dark, rich mille-feuille of caramelised apples is as delicious as it is unique. Thin sliced apples, layered with sugar and citrus, slowly cooked so that they retain their shape but melt into a dense all-apple cake that is irresistible. Take your time and you'll get it right on the first try.

Although the ingredients list is short, this does take time to assemble. An extra pair of hands to peel and slice the apples makes the process go much faster. Assemble it the morning of the day before you wish to serve it, or even the day before that. Jean-Georges serves it with Green Apple Sorbet (page 175), a piece of Sableuse (page 167), and a dollop of crème fraîche or sour cream, but it's great solo.

SERVES 14 – 20

APPLE CONFIT

500g/1lb sugar

5 oranges

15 Granny Smith apples

1 Melt half the sugar in a sauté pan over medium heat, stirring only occasionally, until it bubbles and turns golden brown. Immediately pour it into a standard 23 × 12-cm/9 × 5-in loaf tin, or a 8-cm/3-in-deep, 23-cm/9-in round cake pan. Swirl the melted sugar around so that it coats the bottom, and set it aside. It will harden while you prepare the oranges and apples.

2 Use a zester to remove the orange zest in long, thin strips. Place the zest in a saucepan with water to cover. Bring to the boil, then cook for 1 minute. Drain, then refresh under cold running water for a minute or two. Drain again.

3 Peel the apples, then halve and core them. Cut them by hand or with a mandoline into even slices about 3mm/⅛in thick; keep the slices neatly stacked.

4 Using only flat pieces (discard the rounded ends), place a layer of apples neatly in the bottom of the loaf tin. Cover with another layer, keeping the layers as level as possible, and pressing down to even them out. Sprinkle with a bit of the remaining sugar, then some of the zest. Repeat, adding sugar and zest every 2 or 3 layers.

5 When you get to the top of the tin, keep the lines straight and continue to build layers beyond the top, going about 8–10cm/3–4in above the tin. Cover the top with plastic, then wrap the whole tin in aluminum foil. Place it in a shallow tray – it will drip – and refrigerate at least overnight and preferably for 24 hours.

6 Drain the juice from the tray (you can reserve it for sorbet or other uses), then unwrap the tin. Drain the excess liquid, then wrap the pan in a double layer of aluminum foil. Place the tin in a large, deep roasting pan, and fill the roasting pan with water halfway up the sides of the loaf tin. Bake at 150°C/300°F/gas 2 for 5 hours, then check: the confit is done when all the apple slices are dark brown, it has shrunk to fill only about $^3/_4$ of the mould, and a thin-bladed knife pierces it easily. Cooking time is usually between 5 and 6$^1/_2$ hours; check and replenish the water bath (use boiling water) as necessary.

7 Unwrap the confit, cool, then chill for several hours, up to 2 days. Slice thinly and serve.

If there is a more elegant dessert made with such ease, I don't know it. This is a mélange of brilliantly simple techniques – foolproof, I assure you – that produces a shiny, bright, gorgeous peach.

You can use an equal number of dried apricots for the sauce; reconstitute them in warm water for 10 minutes before beginning.

MAKES 4 SERVINGS

LACQUERED PEACHES

6 apricots, about 250g/½lb, stoned

1 vanilla pod, split lengthwise

225g/7oz sugar

4 large peaches (about 750g/1½lb)

Juice of 1 lime

Ginger Ice Cream (page 182), optional

1 Combine the apricots with 470ml/16fl oz water, the vanilla pod, and half the sugar in a small saucepan. Boil until very tender, for at least 15 minutes. Cool. Preheat the oven to 230°C/450°F/gas 8.

2 Meanwhile, bring a pot of water to the boil and submerge the peaches (one or two at a time) in the water until their skins loosen, for about 30 seconds. Drop into a bowl of iced water and peel when they cool down.

3 Put the apricots in a blender with about 4 tablespoons of their poaching liquid. Process until the mixture is very smooth, adding a little more liquid, if necessary, to allow the machine to work.

4 Place the remaining half of the sugar in a heavy-bottomed saucepan and turn the heat to high. Cook, shaking the pan occasionally, until the sugar melts and just turns brown. Reduce the heat to low, stand back to avoid spatters, and pour in the apricot purée. Add the lime juice and cook, stirring, until the ingredients are blended.

5 Place the peaches on a large rimmed baking tray, preferably nonstick. Spoon all of the glaze over them and place in the oven. Bake for 10 minutes, then baste with the juice; most of it will already have formed a glaze. Bake for 5 minutes more, then serve, spooning any remaining sauce over the peaches. Serve on their own or, if you like, with Ginger Ice Cream.

Grilled peaches in a yellow sabayon make a great last-minute dessert, yet one impressive enough to be served at the four-star Jean-Georges.

SERVES 4 – 6

Make the sabayon in advance – up to a day, even two – if you like.

PEACH GRATIN

3 egg yolks

4 tablespoons sugar

125ml/4fl oz champagne or other sparkling wine

4 large peaches, about 175g/6oz each

2½ tablespoons butter

125g/4oz currants, berries, or cherries, stoned

125ml/4fl oz double cream

1 Combine the egg yolks, sugar and champagne in a saucepan, and bring to the boil over high heat, whisking all the while. When the mixture foams up, continue to beat for 1 minute. Cool, then refrigerate. (If you're serving the dish right away, cool by placing the bowl in a larger bowl filled with ice and water; stir occasionally.)

2 Bring a pot of water to the boil and submerge the peaches (one or two at a time) in the water until their skins loosen, for about 30 seconds. Drop into a bowl of iced water and peel when they cool down. Pit and slice.

3 Melt the butter in a large nonstick frying pan over high heat. When the foam subsides, add the peaches; brown them very lightly, just for 1 to 2 minutes, then turn over and brown the other sides, again for just a minute.

4 Arrange the peaches in a gratin dish or in 4 or 6 small bowls; garnish with the currants. Preheat the grill.

5 Whip the cream until it barely holds a soft peak, then stir it into the sabayon. Spoon the sabayon over the peaches and run the dish(es) under the grill until the sauce is nicely browned on top. Serve immediately.

If those who attack French chefs for using Asian ingredients in traditional French foods tasted this dish, they'd faint.

SERVES 4 – 6

The addition of star anise converts a homely French dessert – essentially sweet pancake batter and fruit – into something exotic.

PEAR CLAFOUTI WITH STAR ANISE

1 vanilla pod, split lengthwise, one half reserved for another use

3 eggs

125g/4oz granulated sugar

5 tablespoons flour, plus a little for dusting the pan

150ml/5fl oz cream, crème fraîche, or plain yogurt

150ml/5fl oz milk

3 star anise, ground in a coffee grinder

Pinch salt

1 teaspoon butter

4 ripe pears, about 175g/6oz each, peeled

1 teaspoon pear eau du vie or brandy (optional)

Caster sugar

1 Preheat the oven to 180°C/350°F/gas 4. Scrape the tiny seeds from one half of the vanilla pod.

2 Beat the eggs with the vanilla seeds until frothy. Add the granulated sugar and beat with a whisk or hand or electric mixer until foamy and fairly thick.

3 Add the flour and continue to beat until thick and smooth. Add the cream, crème fraîche or yogurt, milk, anise and salt. Leave to rest while you prepare the pears and the baking dish.

4 Choose a 23 × 13 × 5-cm/9 × 5 × 2-in gratin dish or a 25-cm/10-in round deep pie plate or porcelain dish and smear it with the butter. Dust it with flour, rotating the pan so the flour sticks to all the butter, then inverting the dish to get rid of excess flour.

5 Cut the pears into sixths or eighths, remove the cores, and layer them attractively in the bottom of the dish. Sprinkle them with eau du vie, if you like. Pour the batter over, leaving just a little of the tops of the pears peeking through.

6 Bake for 20 minutes, or until the clafouti is nicely browned on top and a knife inserted into it comes out clean. Sift some caster sugar over it and serve warm or at room temperature.

This is one of those desserts whose appearance belies its ease of preparation.

The crêpes are the only real challenge, but there's enough batter here to make plenty of mistakes and still come out on top. Rice flour can be found in natural foods stores and many supermarkets.

SERVES 4

CRISPY RICE CREPES WITH RASPBERRIES AND COCONUT

5 tablespoons rice flour

1 tablespoon butter, melted

2 egg whites

2 tablespoons caster sugar, plus more for dusting the crêpes

300g/10oz raspberries

250ml/9fl oz cream

4 tablespoons shredded, unsweetened coconut

1 tablespoon coconut-flavoured (such as Malibu) or plain rum

1 Preheat the oven to 180°C/350°F/gas 4. Mix together 190ml/6fl oz water, the rice flour, butter and egg whites in a medium bowl to make a thin batter. Heat an 20-cm/8-in frying pan, preferably nonstick, over medium-high heat. Pour about 2 tablespoons batter into the pan and swirl it around, pouring out the excess. Cook until firm but not browned, then flip, using a spatula (and your fingers if necessary). Remove when solid but not browned, then cool for a moment and cut into 4 wedges. Repeat to make a total of 4 crepes (16 wedges).

2 Place the crêpe pieces on a baking tray and use a strainer or sifter to make an even but thin layer of caster sugar on them. Bake for 10 to 15 minutes, or until dry and lightly browned.

3 Meanwhile, pick out about a quarter of the nicest raspberries and set them aside. Crush the remaining berries with the back of a spoon to make a rough purée. Whip the cream with 2 tablespoons of caster sugar until nice and thick but not at all stiff; it should not even hold soft peaks. Stir in the coconut and the rum until well combined.

4 To assemble, place a piece of crêpe on a plate, then spread over a little cream, then some of the raspberry purée. Repeat: crêpe, cream, purée, crêpe, cream, purée, crêpe. Top the last crêpe with a few raspberries, some of the juice from the purée, and a little caster sugar. Repeat to make 4 plates and serve.

While pastry chef Eric Hubert was working at Patria, the New York Latino restaurant, he learned to make the classic *tres leches* – a custard made from three kinds of milk.

Combining the custard with puff pastry in a French dessert results in a not-your-usual kiwi tart.

SERVES 4

KIWI TART

Eight 8-cm/3-in circles puff pastry (page 184), refrigerated, about 3mm/⅛in thick

250ml/9fl oz evaporated milk

2 vanilla pods, split, seeds scraped out and pods reserved

250ml/9fl oz coconut milk

250ml/9fl oz sweetened condensed milk

Caster sugar

4 ripe kiwis, peeled and thinly sliced

1 Preheat the oven to 180°C/350°F/gas 4. Poke the puff pastry circles all over with a fork, then bake them for about 15 minutes, or until golden brown. Remove and cool on a rack. You can do this a few hours in advance as long as the weather is dry.

2 Combine the evaporated milk and the vanilla pods and seeds in a medium saucepan over medium heat and bring to the boil, whisking frequently to make sure it doesn't burn. As soon as it boils, add the coconut milk and continue to whisk and cook. As soon as the mixture boils again, add the condensed milk. Bring to the boil and cook, stirring frequently, until it is reduced to a thick beige syrup, about 20 minutes. Cool over iced water or in the refrigerator.

3 Preheat the grill. Place the puff pastry circles on a baking sheet (do this in batches if necessary) and dust them with caster sugar. Run the circles under the grill until the sugar melts and browns a little, just a minute or so.

4 Remove the vanilla pods from the milk mixture. Spoon a bit of the milk mixture onto a circle, then top with another circle, then more sauce and, finally, some overlapping slices of kiwi. Repeat to make 4 tarts. Serve, or refrigerate for up to 2 hours before serving.

Serve this sweet-and-sour dessert hot, or at least warm, and don't taste the orange-zest mixture raw, because you'll throw it away – it tastes awful.

Nevertheless, this a good example of the whole being greater

MAKES 4 SMALL TARTS (in this case, much greater) than the sum of its parts.

 # RHUBARB TARTS

¼ recipe refrigerated puff pastry (page 184), about 250g/½lb

Zest of 5 oranges

2½ tablespoons butter

1 egg

1 teaspoon cornflour

3 or 4 stalks rhubarb, strings removed and minced

4 tablespoons brown sugar

Caster sugar

1 Let the puff pastry sit at room temperature for at least 10 minutes before attempting to roll it. Sprinkle a board with flour and roll out the dough into a rectangle, turning and flouring frequently but sparingly. When the dough is 3mm/⅛in thick, cut it into four 10-cm/4-in circles, using a small plate or saucer as your guide. You will have plenty of leftover dough; freeze or refrigerate it for another use.

2 Mince the orange zest very finely (you can use a small food processor for this if you like); there should be about 4 tablespoons. Place the zest in a fine strainer and run hot water over it for about 15 seconds, then squeeze dry.

3 Cream together 2 tablespoons of the butter, the egg and cornflour, then add the zest. Place in the refrigerator, or over a bowl of iced water, whisking occasionally, until slightly stiffened. Meanwhile, preheat the oven to 200°C/400°F/gas 6.

4 Place the puff pastry disks on a parchment-lined baking sheet. Spread a quarter of the orange zest mixture on each, leaving a 2-cm/½-in border. Arrange the rhubarb nicely over this, then sprinkle with brown sugar and dot with the remaining butter.

5 Bake for about 15 minutes, or until the bottom is golden brown and the rhubarb is tender. Sift some caster sugar over the tarts and serve warm.

Once you've made (or bought) puff pastry – which freezes well – this lovely stack of berries, crisp crust, and whipped cream is easy to make.

And, despite its simplicity (or maybe because of it), it's among my favourites of the many splendid desserts created by Eric Hubert.

RED BERRY MILLE-FEUILLE

¼ recipe puff pastry (page 184) about 250g/½lb

375ml/13fl oz cream

2½ tablespoons sugar

150g/5oz raspberries

150g/5oz strawberries, hulled and chopped to about the same size as the raspberries

150g/5oz blueberries or blackberries (chop blackberries as you did strawberries)

Caster sugar

1 Let the puff pastry sit at room temperature for at least 10 minutes before attempting to roll it. Sprinkle a board with flour and roll out the dough into a rectangle, turning and flouring frequently but sparingly. When the dough is 3mm/⅛in thick, trim it to about 25 × 50cm/10 × 20in and place it on a greaseproof paper-lined baking tray. Refrigerate for 30 minutes while you preheat the oven to 180°C/350°F/gas 4.

2 Poke the pastry all over with a fork, then bake for about 15 minutes, or until golden brown. Remove and cool on a rack. (You can do this a few hours in advance as long as the weather is dry. You can even do it a day in advance; store the puff pastry in a closed container, or recrisp it briefly in the oven before assembling the mille-feuille.)

3 About an hour before you're ready to serve the mille-feuille, set the bowl and whisk for the cream in the refrigerator or in a bowl of iced water to chill.

4 Cut the baked puff pastry into 16 strips, each about 5 × 12cm/2 × 5in (this allows plenty of room for error). Save all the trimmings and crumble them into a bowl.

5 Whisk the cream in the chilled bowl until it is fairly stiff – it should hold well-defined peaks. Whisk in 1 tablespoon of the sugar.

6 Combine the fruit in a bowl with the remaining sugar; mix well.

7 Spread a small amount of whipped cream on each of four plates. Top it with a piece of the pastry, then spread with a little more whipped cream and a

few berries. Top with another piece of pastry, and repeat until four pieces of pastry enclose three layers of berries and cream.

8 If any whipped cream remains, spread it along the sides of the mille-feuilles and sprinkle with some of the reserved puff pastry crumbs.

9 Serve immediately or refrigerate for up to 60 minutes. Garnish with any remaining berries.

This classic French biscuit is prepared in two steps. You make a biscuit and crumble it. Stir more butter into the crumbled biscuit, then make biscuits of *that* dough. The result is so delicate you can barely pick them up and they melt in your mouth.

Serve, if you like, with Peppered Poached Apricots (page 153) and any ice cream, or with Warm Fruit Compôte (page 152).

MAKES 12 OR MORE
8-CM/3-IN BISCUITS

PETIT BEURRE

190g/6½oz plain flour

90g/3oz almond flour (see Note)

130g/4½oz butter, softened

115g/4oz sugar

1 Preheat the oven to 200°C/400°F/gas 6. Combine the flour, almond flour, 50g/2oz of the butter, and the sugar in a medium bowl. Using your hands, mix together, squeezing the mixture between your fingers. It will hold together, but barely.

2 Press the dough onto a nonstick baking tray, in a rectangle about 1.2cm/½in thick. Bake for 15 minutes, or until pale brown and cracking at the edges.

3 As soon as the biscuit is cool – it will harden – use your fingers to crumble it into the bowl of a standing mixer with a paddle attachment. Add the remaining butter and mix for about 5 minutes, or until the butter is completely incorporated and you can press the dough together with your hand; again, it will be crumbly.

4 Roll the dough out on a piece of greasproof paper, using another piece of greaseproof paper on top, until you have a rectangle about 23 × 35cm/ 9 × 14in; it need not be perfect.

5 Slide the parchment onto a baking tray, and use a 7-cm/3-in tartlet cutter to mark 12 cookies; do not try to separate them. Bake for about 10 minutes, or until the biscuits are beautifully browned. Remove from the oven, then recut the biscuits, still leaving them in one piece.

6 Cool for at least 30 minutes before separating into individual bis cuits, but handle very carefully. The leftover pieces are wonderful crumbled over ice cream, Peppered Poached Apricots or Warm Fruit Compôte.

NOTE:
Almond flour can be purchased from specialist baking catalogues or suppliers. Or you can pulse peeled, blanched almonds in a food processor until powdery.

Florentines are traditional brittle biscuits which, given the Vong treatment by pastry chef Serge Decrauzat, wind up sparkling with flavour.

These are fun and easy to make (a good baking project for kids, because the dough cannot be overworked), and the crystallised ginger adds a spark. Serve as an accompaniment to ice cream or crumble them on top.

MAKES ABOUT 20
BISCUITS

SESAME FLORENTINES

2 tablespoons vegetable, grapeseed or other neutral-flavoured oil

4 tablespoons cream

2½ tablespoons sugar

25g/1oz butter

1 tablespoon honey

4 tablespoons flour

2 tablespoons minced crystallised ginger

75g/2½oz sesame seeds

1 Brush a sheet of greaseproof or wax paper, about 30 × 60cm/1 × 2ft, with the oil. Preheat the oven to 200°C/400°F/gas 6.

2 Combine the cream, sugar, butter and honey in a small saucepan and cook over medium heat, stirring, until the mixture bubbles. Reduce the heat a bit and continue to cook, stirring, for about 5 minutes, until the colour changes to a light brown.

3 Stir in the flour, ginger and sesame seeds and cook, stirring constantly with a whisk, for 5 minutes. You want to brown the mixture a little more, and also to remove the raw taste of the flour.

4 Scrape the mixture, which will be very thick and sticky, onto the greaseproof paper, then fold the paper onto itself; be careful, because it is still hot. Press down on it with your hands (it is impossible to be too rough with this dough), then roll it, through the paper, with a rolling pin.

5 Turn the dough as it cools, and roll it as thinly as you can. After a few minutes, it will hold its shape and become less sticky.

6 Place the thin dough on its greaseproof paper onto a baking tray and bake for about 12 minutes. It is done when it becomes even more brown, tiny holes appear on its surface, and it bubbles slightly. Remove the tray from the oven.

7 If you want traditional diamond or other shapes, cut it with a lightly oiled knife (just rub the knife with some oil) after about 2 minutes. If you don't care about shapes, let the mixture cool, then break it into pieces.

Tuiles – thin, 'tile'-shaped biscuits – are easy to assemble, but they are a little tricky to bake and shape. The ideal is to have two or even three baking trays (nonstick are best), and to rotate them in and out of the oven; the tuiles must cool for a minute or so on the sheets before moving them. To make the traditional tile shape, drape the still-hot wafers over a thick rolling pin or bottle; to make little cups, drape them over the backs of small glasses; or cool them flat.

Naturally, the tuiles Jean-Georges makes now are a little different than those he grew up with, but Lemon Tuiles are more or less traditional. Once you've mastered these, experiment with your own flavourings.

MAKES 12 OR MORE

THREE UNUSUAL TUILES

TWO-PEPPER TUILES

100g/3½oz brown sugar

40g/1½oz flour

1 teaspoon coarsely ground black pepper

1 teaspoon Szechwan peppercorns, cracked with the bottom of a pot and minced with a knife

2 tablespoons butter, melted

90ml/3fl oz coconut milk

COCONUT TUILES

40g/1½oz flour

100g/3½oz brown sugar

2 tablespoons butter, melted

90ml/3fl oz coconut milk

LEMON TUILES

115g/4oz caster sugar

25g/1oz flour

1 tablespoon butter, melted

2 tablespoons lemon juice

1 Preheat the oven to 200°C/400°F/gas 6. Combine the dry ingredients, then stir in the melted butter and any other liquid; stir until smooth. Note: if you are making Lemon Tuiles, the batter must be refrigerated for 24 hours before baking.

2 Place about a teaspoon of batter on a nonstick baking tray and spread it out as thinly as possible with a small spatula or the back of a spoon. Repeat until the tray is full. Bake for about 7 minutes, or until the tuiles are lacy.

3 Remove the baking tray from the oven and leave the tuiles to rest for a minute. Remove them with a thin spatula or butter knife and drape over a thick rolling pin, soda can, wine bottle or similar object until cool. Serve within a day.

SIMPLE GOOD FOOD

Sableuse is a nineteenth-century Parisian butter cake recipe that Jean-Georges has tinkered with. A light, airy yet rich cake, it's unusual not only in the proportions of ingredients but in the mixing method and the inclusion of cornflour. When he began breaking eggs to make this cake, he said, 'You'll never make a traditional pound cake again.' He was right.

Serve with Warm Fruit Compôte (page 152), Apple Confit (page 154), or any ice cream. And flavour the sableuse batter, if you like, as you would a pound cake – with vanilla, ginger, or lemon.

MAKES ONE 23 X 13CM/9 X 5IN CAKE, 8 TO 12 PORTIONS

SABLEUSE

9 egg yolks

1 egg

200g/7oz sugar

250g/8½oz butter

60g/2oz flour

60g/2oz cornflour

1 Combine the egg yolks, whole egg and sugar in the bowl of an electric mixer and beat on medium speed for 20 minutes (imagine doing this by hand!). The mixture will become almost white and very thick.

2 Meanwhile, melt the butter and let it cool a bit. Butter a 23 × 13-cm/ 9 × 5-in loaf tin; cut a piece of greaseproof or wax paper and fit it into the bottom of the pan. Butter the paper. Preheat the oven to 190°C/375°F/ gas 5.

3 When you've mixed the eggs for 20 minutes, beat in the flour and cornstarch at low speed, just until combined. Add the butter and beat again just until combined. Turn the speed up for 10 seconds, then turn off the machine.

4 Pour the mixture into the prepared tin and wrap completely and tightly in 1 layer of aluminum foil – do not make the foil too thick on the bottom. Bake for 45 to 50 minutes. Unwrap; when the cake is done, the top will be nicely browned but quite light and tender.

5 Immediately invert the pan onto a piece of buttered paper or a flat platter. Lift off the tin, then cover the cake with clingfilm and cool. Slice carefully – it's delicate.

Undercooked chocolate cake? 'It was a mistake,' says Jean-Georges, but is now one of the most popular (and copied) desserts in New York. When you cut into the biscuit-like crust with your spoon the warm creamy pudding-like centre oozes out. This brings out the kid in everyone; but the barely sweet nature of the chocolate batter is too sophisticated for most children.

It's best when served with a scoop of vanilla or caramel ice cream.

The cakes can be prepared ahead of time, refrigerated, and then brought back to room temperature before baking.

MAKES 4 INDIVIDUAL CAKES

WARM, SOFT CHOCOLATE CAKE

125g/4oz butter, plus some for buttering the moulds

125g/4oz bittersweet chocolate, preferably Valrhona

2 eggs

2 egg yolks

4 tablespoons sugar

2 teaspoons flour, plus more for dusting

1 In the top of a double boiler set over simmering water, heat the butter and chocolate together until the chocolate is almost completely melted. While that's heating, beat together the eggs, yolks and sugar with a whisk or electric beater until light and thick.

2 Beat together the melted chocolate and butter; it should be quite warm. Pour in the egg mixture, then quickly beat in the flour, until just combined.

3 Butter and lightly flour four 125g/4oz moulds, custard cups, or ramekins. Tap out the excess flour, then butter and flour them again. Divide the batter among the moulds. (At this point you can refrigerate the desserts until you are ready to eat, for up to several hours; bring them back to room temperature before baking.)

4 Preheat the oven to 230°C/450°F/gas 8. Bake the moulds on a tray for 6 to 7 minutes; the centre will still be quite soft, but the sides will be set.

5 Invert each mould onto a plate and leave it sit for about 10 seconds. Unmould by lifting up one corner of the mould; the cake will fall out onto the plate. Serve immediately.

An all-purpose chocolate batter that makes beautifully high, barely sweet soufflés as well as light, airy chocolate mousse.

Jean-Georges's pastry chef Eric Hubert serves this with raspberries cooked as in Warm Fruit Compôte (page 152).

SERVES 4

CHOCOLATE SOUFFLE OR CHOCOLATE MOUSSE

175g/6oz bittersweet chocolate, chopped

Butter

4 tablespoons granulated sugar, plus some for the moulds

4 eggs, separated

1/8 teaspoon lemon juice

Caster sugar

1 Gently melt the chocolate in a small saucepan over extremely low heat or gently simmering water; cool.

2 Rub each of 4 ramekins, about 8cm/3in wide by 5cm/2in high, with a little butter, then sprinkle them with granulated sugar; tap out the excess sugar. If you're making soufflés, preheat the oven to 200°C/400°F/gas 6.

3 Beat the whites until foamy, then add the lemon juice. As the egg whites rise, add the granulated sugar, a little at a time. Beat until stiff but not dry.

4 Stir the yolks into the cooled chocolate. Whisk in about one-quarter of the whites, then pour the mixture back into the whites and fold it in gently but thoroughly.

5 Spoon the mixture into the moulds, then tap each of them against the work surface. Run your thumb along the inside of each, wiping the rim and top 3mm/1/8in clean so the mixture will move toward the centre a bit. At this point they can sit, refrigerated, for up to an hour. Or you can chill them and serve them as chocolate mousse.

6 Bake for about 10 minutes, or until puffed up and dry on top; the inside should remain quite moist. Sprinkle with caster sugar and serve immediately.

This recipe isn't all that different from traditional crème caramel, but it has the distinctive – and easily added – flavour of coconut.

SERVES 4

COCONUT CREME CARAMEL

125g/4oz sugar

4 eggs

125ml/4fl oz milk

375ml/13fl oz coconut milk

1 vanilla pod, split, or 1 teaspoon vanilla extract

1   Place half the sugar in a small, heavy-bottomed saucepan and turn the heat to medium-high. Cook, shaking the pan occasionally, until the sugar melts and turns a nice shade of brown. Immediately pour it into 4 small ramekins, swirling to distribute. Preheat the oven to 150°C/300°F/gas 2.

2   Combine the remaining sugar with the eggs and whisk until well dissolved. Add the milks and the seeds from the vanilla pod (reserve the pod for another use) or extract and whisk briefly to combine.

3   Place the ramekins in a baking tin containing about 1.2cm/½in of water, then pour one-quarter of the milk mixture into each ramekin. Cover the tin tightly with aluminum foil, then bake for about 45 minutes, or until the custards are just set on the outside but still somewhat jiggly in the middle.

4   Remove the ramekins from the baking pan, then cool and chill. When you're ready to serve, run a knife around the edge of each of the custards, then invert onto plates.

Pierre Schutz, the chef at Vong who created this dish, serves it with Bitter Chocolate Sorbet (page 174).

Although you may find the idea of a soft caramel dessert intimidating, this is as easy to make as brownies.

This recipe makes four very small servings, but, believe me, it's

enough; the stuff is intense.

SOFT CARAMEL WITH SALTED PEANUTS

25g/1oz shelled and salted peanuts

25g/1oz shelled and salted pistachios (or use all peanuts)

2½ tablespoons salted butter

150g/5oz sugar

90ml/3fl oz milk

90ml/3fl oz cream

1　Preheat the oven to 180°C/350°F/gas 4. Toast the nuts in a dry frying pan over medium heat for 5 minutes, shaking the pan occasionally.

2　Melt the butter in a 2.5–3.5-l/4–6-pint saucepan over medium heat. Stir in the sugar and cook, stirring, for about 2 minutes, or until the sugar is completely dissolved.

3　Stir in the milk and boil it, still over medium heat, stirring occasionally, for about 10 minutes. You'll know that you are nearing the end of the cooking period when the mixture begins to turn brown. At that point, stir almost constantly to prevent burning.

4　When the mixture becomes caramel-coloured, stir in the cream and reduce the heat to very low. Stir constantly; the mixture will look bubbly at first, but will quickly become smooth. Remove from the heat; if the mixture seems too thick, thin it with a little more cream.

5　Stir in the nuts and cool to room temperature before serving, in ramekins or small bowls. (Or refrigerate, covered, for up to 2 days. Bring to room temperature and stir before serving.)

Traditional pots de crème are intentionally bland, flavoured with vanilla and little else. They're good, but their almost-blank canvas gives Jean-Georges plenty of opportunity to play around with flavour combinations.

SERVES 6

Here are two possibilities; use the same proportions and techniques to make pots de crème flavoured with espresso, thyme, lemon verbena, or almost anything else you can think of.

LEMONGRASS POTS DE CRÈME

2 stalks lemongrass

470ml/16fl oz milk

6 egg yolks

125g/4oz sugar

1 Trim the lemongrass, then chop it finely. Place it in a small saucepan with the milk and turn the heat to medium-high. Bring to the boil, reduce the heat, and simmer for about 5 minutes. Cover, reduce the heat to its absolute minimum, and leave to rest for 10 minutes. Preheat the oven to 140°C/275°F/gas 1.

2 Meanwhile, beat the egg yolks with the sugar until thick and well blended. Strain the milk through a muslin or fine strainer; then pour it, gradually, into the egg-sugar mixture, whisking all the while.

3 Divide the mixture among 6 ramekins or espresso cups and place them in a baking tray. Add enough water to the tray to come to within 2.5cm/1in of the tops of the ramekins. Cover the tray tightly with aluminum foil, then bake for 20 minutes. When done, the puddings will be firm on the edges but still jiggly in the middle. Replace the cover and bake a few minutes more if necessary, or remove if done. Serve warm or chilled.

Jean-Georges loves licorice – he even uses licorice sticks as skewers – and rightly so.

Both Licorice Ice Cream (page 181) and these simple pots de

crème have been popular at Vong since its opening.

STAR ANISE POTS DE CREME

470ml/16fl oz milk

2 tablespoons broken star anise

6 egg yolks

125g/4oz sugar

1 Heat the milk and star anise together until almost boiling. Reduce the heat to low and cook for 3 minutes. Cover and leave to sit over very low heat for about 5 minutes. Preheat the oven to 140°C/275°F/gas 1.

2 Meanwhile, beat the egg yolks with the sugar until thick and well blended.

3 Put the milk mixture in a blender; whir for 30 seconds. Strain through muslin or other fine strainer. Gradually beat into the egg yolks until well combined.

4 Pour into 6 small ramekins or small pots, and place them in a baking pan. Add enough water to the pan to come to within 2.5cm/1in of the tops of the ramekins. Tightly cover the pan with aluminum foil, then bake for 20 minutes. When done, the puddings will be firm on the edges but still jiggly in the middle. Replace the cover and bake for a few minutes more if necessary, or remove if done. Serve warm or chilled.

Because it is so low in fat, chocolate sorbet has a very limited storage life; I recommend that you make it and eat it the same day.

In fact, it's at its best if you make it while you're eating dinner. Remove it from the machine, and serve it without ever placing it in the freezer.

BITTER CHOCOLATE SORBET

1 vanilla pod or 1 teaspoon vanilla extract

130g/4½oz cocoa powder, Valrhona if you have it, or any other brand if you don't

125g/4oz sugar

1 Bring 470ml/16fl oz water to the boil, then cool slightly.

2 Split the vanilla pod and scrape the tiny seeds from half of it; save the remaining vanilla pod, wrapped in aluminum foil, for another use.

3 Combine the seeds or extract in a bowl with the cocoa, sugar, and water, and whisk until well blended. Strain into another bowl and chill; you can keep the mixture, refrigerated, for a few days.

4 Freeze in an ice cream machine according to the manufacturer's instructions and eat as soon as possible.

This is a lightly sweetened, subtle sorbet that Eric Hubert, pastry chef at Jean-Georges, serves with his Apple Confit (page 154).

It has only one disadvantage: it must be frozen immediately, or it will turn brown instead of its distinctively lovely pale green. Like all sorbets, it should be eaten as soon as possible after freezing.

SERVES 4 – 6

GREEN APPLE SORBET

125g/4oz sugar

8 Granny Smith apples

Juice of 1 lemon

1 Place the sugar in a small saucepan with 125ml/4fl oz water. Turn the heat to high and cook, stirring, until the sugar dissolves, just a minute or two. Chill by placing the saucepan in a bowl of ice.

2 Wash the apples and put them through a juicer. Combine the juice with 125ml/4fl oz of the sugar syrup and the lemon juice.

3 Freeze in an ice cream maker according to the manufacturer's directions.

For years, I'd admired Jean-Georges's coconut sorbet – first at Vong, then at JoJo, and finally at Jean-Georges. But it was only when we finally made it together that I regretted not asking him for the recipe sooner, because it is *so* easy to make at home.

SERVES 4

Like all sorbets, this is best eaten the day it is made, but it keeps better than most; even three-day-old coconut sorbet is quite good.

COCONUT SORBET

2 cans coconut milk, each 400ml/ 14fl oz

170g/6oz sugar

1 tablespoon rum, preferably coconut-flavoured rum, such as Malibu

1 Combine the coconut milk and sugar in a saucepan over medium heat; whisk until the sugar dissolves. Stir in the rum.

2 Chill, then freeze in an ice cream maker according to the manufacturer's directions.

Shop-bought frozen yogurt is indistinguishable from low-fat ice cream. But Vong pastry chef Serge

Decrauzat believes it should have tang, and this one does.

Perfect with sweet fruit desserts, such as Warm Fruit Compôte

(page 152), and easy as can be.

LEMON YOGURT SORBET

125g/4oz sugar

470ml/16fl oz plain yogurt

4 tablespoons lemon juice

Grated zest of 2 lemons

1 Place the sugar in a small saucepan with 250ml/9fl oz of water. Heat, stirring occasionally, until the sugar dissolves. Cool (if you want to work fast, place the pot in a large bowl of iced water).

2 Combine the sugar syrup with the yogurt, lemon juice and zest.

3 Chill, then freeze in an ice cream machine according to the manufacturer's directions.

Traditionally, crème glacée contains no milk, but Jean-Georges adds a little yogurt for added tang.

That, plus the lime flavour, makes this a distinctive sweet-and-sour

dessert.

LIME CREME GLACEE

About 1 dozen limes

125g/4oz sugar

60g/2oz butter

6 eggs

125ml/4fl oz plain yogurt

1 Grate the zest from 4 of the limes; mince and combine it with the sugar and butter in a small saucepan. Turn the heat to medium-low and cook, stirring occasionally, until the mixture liquefies.

2 Squeeze enough of the limes to make 190ml/6fl oz juice. Whisk into the butter-sugar mixture until well combined. Stir in the eggs, then the yogurt, and whisk for a minute or so. Strain the mixture through a fine sieve.

3 Chill, then freeze in an ice cream machine according to the manufacturer's directions.

Jean-Georges changes ice cream flavours the way others change clothes – to suit his mood.

He'll use any number of spice mixtures. This is a favourite: complex

and nearly – but not quite – hot.

SPICE ICE CREAM

2.5cm/1in cinnamon stick

1 teaspoon mace

1 teaspoon freshly grated nutmeg

1 teaspoon pepper

1 teaspoon coriander

470ml/16fl oz milk

2 vanilla pods, split, seeds scraped out and pods reserved for another use

6 egg yolks

125g/4oz sugar

1 Combine the cinnamon, mace, nutmeg, pepper and coriander in a dry frying pan over medium heat and cook, shaking, until aromatic, for a minute or so. Cool slightly, then grind to a powder.

2 Rinse a medium saucepan and leave it wet. Add the milk, vanilla seeds and 1 tablespoon of the spice mixture. Turn the heat to medium-high and bring just to the boil, stirring.

3 Beat the yolks and sugar together until thick and slightly lightened in colour. Stir about 125ml/4fl oz of the hot milk into the yolk mixture and beat; then stir the warmed egg mixture back into the milk. Heat, stirring constantly, until thick. The mixture is ready when it thickly coats the back of a spoon, and a line drawn with your finger remains intact. Taste and add more of the spice mixture, if you like; then cool and strain through a fine sieve.

4 Chill, then freeze in an ice cream machine according to the manufacturer's directions.

By itself, cardamom ice cream is good. Mixed with coffee (a traditional Middle Eastern combination), it's even better.

MAKES ABOUT 600ML/1 PINT,
AT LEAST 4 PORTIONS

CARDAMOM-COFFEE ICE CREAM

470ml/16fl oz milk

2 vanilla pods, split, seeds scraped out and pods reserved for another use

1 tablespoon cardamom pods or 2 teaspoons ground cardamom

2 tablespoons finely ground espresso beans

6 egg yolks

125g/4oz sugar

1 Rinse a medium saucepan and leave it wet. Add the milk, vanilla seeds, cardamom and coffee. Turn the heat to medium-high and bring just to the boil, stirring.

2 Beat the yolks and sugar together until thick and slightly lightened in colour. Stir about 125ml/4fl oz of the hot milk into the yolk mixture and beat; then stir the warmed egg mixture back into the milk. Heat, stirring constantly, until thick. The mixture is ready when it thickly coats the back of a spoon, and a line drawn with your finger remains intact. Taste and add more seasoning, if you like; then cool and strain through a fine sieve.

3 Chill, then freeze in an ice cream machine according to the manufacturer's directions.

This ice cream is made with real licorice – not the sweet (see page 189). It may not appeal to everyone, but licorice-lovers will find its strength intoxicating.

(see page 189)

MAKES ABOUT 600ML/1 PINT,
AT LEAST 4 PORTIONS

LICORICE ICE CREAM

8cm/3in piece licorice

470ml/16fl oz milk

2 vanilla pods, split, seeds scraped out and pods reserved for another use

6 egg yolks

125g/4oz sugar

1 Chop the licorice coarsely, then grind it as finely as possible in a spice or coffee grinder.

2 Rinse a medium saucepan and leave it wet. Add the milk, vanilla seeds and 1 tablespoon of the ground licorice. Turn the heat to medium-high and bring just to the boil, stirring.

3 Beat the yolks and sugar together until thick and slightly lightened in colour. Stir about 125ml/4fl oz of the hot milk into the yolk mixture and beat; then stir the warmed egg mixture back into the milk. Heat, stirring constantly, until thick. The mixture is ready when it thickly coats the back of a spoon, and a line drawn with your finger remains intact. Taste and add more licorice, if you like; then cool and strain through a fine sieve.

4 Chill, then freeze in an ice cream machine according to the manufacturer's directions.

Fresh ginger is essential here; it produces an ice cream that is slightly hot and explodes with flavour.

MAKES ABOUT 600ML/1 PINT,
AT LEAST 4 PORTIONS

GINGER ICE CREAM

470ml/16fl oz milk

2 vanilla pods, split, seeds scraped out and pods reserved for another use

10-cm/4-in knob of ginger, peeled and roughly chopped

6 egg yolks

125g/4oz sugar

1 Rinse a medium saucepan and leave it wet. Add the milk, vanilla seeds, and ginger. Turn the heat to medium-high and bring just to the boil, stirring. Cover and leave to sit for about 10 minutes.

2 Beat the yolks and sugar together until thick and slightly lightened in colour. Strain the milk, then stir about 125ml/4fl oz of it into the yolk mixture and beat; then stir the warmed egg mixture back into the milk. Heat, stirring constantly, until thick. The mixture is ready when it thickly coats the back of a spoon, and a line drawn with your finger remains intact. Cool and strain through a fine sieve.

3 Chill, then freeze in an ice cream machine according to the manufacturer's directions.

These are essentially sweets, a garnish or post-dessert nibble that you shouldn't count on to fill anyone up.

Having said that, I'll tell you that everyone I know who's sampled these has found them delightful.

Don't make a special trip to buy maple syrup; its contribution is negligible. And, don't bother to make these unless you have a mandoline; the slices must be paper-thin, impossible to cut with a knife.

MAKES 10 SLICES

CRISPY ORANGE SLICES

1 large, thin-skinned juice orange

225g/7oz sugar

1 teaspoon maple syrup (optional)

1 Wash the orange, dry it and use a mandoline to slice it as thinly as you possibly can. The slices should be no more than 2mm/$\frac{1}{16}$in thick.

2 Combine the sugar and 190ml/6fl oz water; add the maple syrup, if you have it. Bring to the boil and stir until the sugar dissolves. Cool a bit, then combine with the orange slices in a bowl. Cover and leave to sit for 2 hours.

3 Preheat the oven to 180°C/350°F/gas 4. Place a sheet of greaseproof paper on a baking sheet or swiss roll tin and arrange the orange slices on it, laying them flat and smoothing them out if necessary. Bake for 5 minutes, then reduce the heat to 110°C/225°F/gas ¼. Bake for 2 hours, reducing the oven heat if the slices seem to be browning. Cool, then remove from the baking sheet. Store in a tin at room temperature for up to several days.

This is the classic crust for many pastries, used here for both savoury dishes, such as Mushroom Tarts with Onion and Walnuts (page 8), and sweet ones, like Red Berry Mille-Feuille (page 162). Making puff pastry is not at all difficult – just remember to chill the pastry well between turns, and to let it warm up a bit if it's difficult to work – but it is time consuming.

The work, however, takes place at easily varied intervals, so it's a nice project for a day when you're around the house doing a variety of things.

MAKES ABOUT 1.1KG/2 ½LB, ENOUGH FOR SEVERAL USES

PUFF PASTRY

460g/1lb flour, plus some for working the dough

1 tablespoon salt

560g/1¼lb butter, 1 stick softened

1 Toss together the flour and salt in a bowl, then mix in the softened butter, rubbing it gently between your fingers until incorporated. Add 250ml/9fl oz cold water and quickly gather the mixture into a ball. Wrap in clingfilm and refrigerate for at least 30 minutes.

2 Place the remaining butter between 2 sheets of foil and pound it into a 15 × 20-cm/6 × 8-in rectangle with a rolling pin or the bottom of a pot.

3 Remove the dough from the refrigerator, flatten it into a disk, and make a shallow 'X' in the middle. Roll each of the segments you've just created out from the centre in a cloverleaf pattern, sprinkling with flour as necessary and leaving the dough slightly higher in the middle than on the petals. Fold the butter so that it is about the same size as the central square, and place it there. One at a time, fold the petals over the butter, stretching them slightly so as to encase the butter, and each other, completely.

4 Pound the package lightly, then square off the sides, then pound again, but not so hard that butter begins to leak out the sides. Roll it out, sprinkling with flour as necessary, continuing to seal the seams with your fingers so the butter does not leak out. Make a 23 × 45-cm/9 × 8-in rectangle, then fold it into thirds. Sprinkle with flour and roll again, repeating the process (it will be easier this time). After the second turn and fold, wrap the dough in clingfilm or a tea towel and leave to rest in a cool place, or the refrigerator.

5 At least 30 minutes later, do 2 more turns. (If the dough is stubborn at first because it is too cold, let it rest at room temperature for 10 minutes before trying again.)

6 Refrigerate for at least 30 minutes, then do 2 more turns. When you're finished, you will have more than 1kg/2lb of puff pastry dough; cut it into halves or quarters, wrap tightly in 2 layers of clingfilm and refrigerate or freeze.

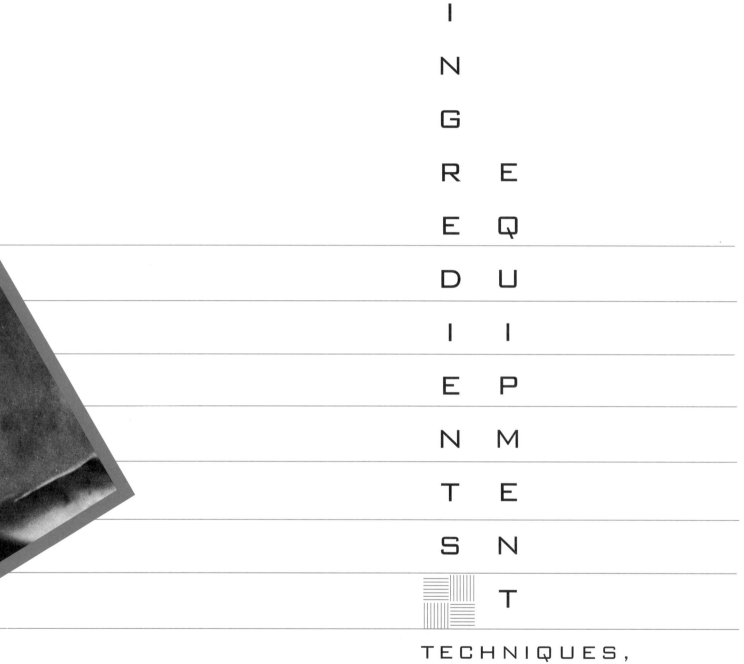

INGREDIENTS

REQUIPMENT

TECHNIQUES,
STOCKS, AND
SAUCES

INGREDIENTS

Many of the Asian elements of Jean-Georges's cooking – lemongrass, coconut milk, even ginger – were considered exotic not too long ago. But these days they are sold in many supermarkets and you can certainly find them in Asian and Chinese markets. Most of them are inexpensive and keep for some time, some with refrigeration, others without.

As for fresh herbs, fresh 'wild' mushrooms (most of which are cultivated these days) and other spices, these too are stocked in many supermarkets, but we've offered substitutes when a particular ingredient might be hard to find.

AMCHUR (also spelled amchoor): a powder made from unripe green mangoes, which are peeled, sliced, sun-dried and ground. It has a pure sour taste and is used much like lemon juice, which is always an acceptable substitute. Covered tightly and stored away from light and heat, it will last indefinitely.

BASIL: now available fresh in most supermarkets year-round, this is among the most fragrant – and fragile – of herbs and almost always best added to dishes at the last minute. Jean-Georges uses a great deal of small-leaved Thai basil (sometimes called sacred basil), which has hints of jasmine, but any basil will do. Store, lightly wrapped in plastic, in the refrigerator, but use as soon as you can.

CARDAMOM: one of Jean-Georges's favourites. Cardamom is available in several forms and several types. You may find whole pods – which may be green, brown-black, or ivory – each of which contain seeds. Or you may find seeds; either is preferable to ground cardamom, which quickly loses its essential oils and, therefore, its flavour. When buying pods, open one and make sure that the seeds are brown-black and slightly sticky.

To use whole pods, crush them lightly with your fingers or the side of a knife, then remove the seeds; you'll get about a teaspoon of seeds for each tablespoon of pods. Unless you're cooking them in a liquid that will later be strained, crush or grind the seeds (in a mortar and pestle or spice grinder) before using. Whole seeds or pods will retain their flavour for at least a year; store in a tightly sealed jar away from light and heat.

CHILLIES: Jean-Georges relies heavily on Thai chillies, which are small (about 2.5cm/1in long), bright red and not super-hot. One or two generally adds a moderate amount of heat to a dish; Jean-Georges rarely makes anything fiery-hot. You can substitute any chilli you like – including dried red chillies – but just make sure you add it gradually to prevent overwhelming the dish with heat. All chillies, even dried ones, should be stored in the refrigerator.

COCONUT MILK: this is *not* the juice from the inside of a coconut, but water pressed through its meat; although it is sweet, it contains no added sugar. Coconut milk is sold in 400ml/14fl oz cans, which can be stored indefinitely; it's inexpensive and of decent quality. If you'd prefer to make your own coconut milk, combine 150g/5oz shredded unsweetened coconut in a blender with 470ml/16fl oz water and carefully blend for 30 seconds or so. Leave for 10 minutes, then press through a strainer.

CORIANDER: Jean-Georges uses both coriander seeds and leaves. He often minces the seeds with a knife to retain a bit of their pleasant crunch. Ground coriander has far less flavour than freshly ground seeds. The leaves are delicate and spoil quickly, so keep them refrigerated, loosely wrapped in plastic bags.

CURRY PASTE: sold in Asian markets, this fiery paste is a blend of spices and chillies which, when refrigerated, keeps for months.

5-SPICE POWDER: a variable Chinese spice mix that does not always contain exactly five spices, but usually has star anise, cinnamon, cloves, Szechwan peppercorns and licorice. Sold ground; like all spices, it should be stored in a covered container away from light and heat.

GALANGAL: this knobby rhizome looks a great deal like ginger, which can fill in nicely. Buy firm roots and store them in plastic bags in the refrigerator. Peel and mince well before using, because it is rather woody.

GINGER: fresh ginger is now available everywhere. Look for a whitish or tan-coloured knobby rhizome that is firm and plump to the touch; it should not be shrivelled, and the interior should be pale gold. Store ginger in a plastic bag in the refrigerator, where it will keep for several weeks.

Usually, ginger is peeled before using. Jean-Georges stores the peels in salt to make ginger salt, a condiment you can sprinkle quite freely.

Dried ginger is an acceptable emergency substitute for fresh ginger.

HERBS (see also individual herbs): a variety of fresh herbs is now sold in all supermarkets, and you should use them whenever possible. Jean-Georges's preference is to use whole or only coarsely chopped leaves, which he believes transmit more flavour than minced leaves.

JUNIPER: the bluish-black berries of the juniper bush, most widely known as the dominant flavouring of gin. Delicious when minced and used sparingly, whether raw or cooked. Store indefinitely at room temperature.

LEMONGRASS: easy to find in Asian or Indian grocery stores if it's not in your supermarket, lemongrass looks like an overgrown, tough spring onion. It has the distinct perfume of lemon, but a decidedly different (and altogether pleasant) flavour. Store it in the refrigerator, where it will keep for weeks.

To use lemongrass, trim the woody ends and peel off the tough outer layer of leaves. If you're cooking it in liquid, smack the stalk with the back end of a knife to help release its flavour. If you're going to eat the lemongrass, peel enough layers away to expose the tender inner core, which is pale ivory, and mince finely.

LICORICE: real licorice is sold dried, as woody sticks, and can be hard to find (check Chinese markets first). The sticks can be infused in liquid or, for more flavour, ground and included in the dish itself. Because licorice is so tough, grinding is a two-step process: first chop coarsely with a knife, then put in a spice grinder.

LIME LEAVES: usually from the tree of the kaffir lime. The leaves are sold fresh or dried, with the former always preferable; they're exquisitely fragrant. Fresh leaves must be refrigerated and used quickly; dried leaves can be stored as bay leaves, and they keep well.

MUSHROOMS: Jean-Georges freely uses mushrooms (including the common, sometimes scorned button mushroom), and frequently in combination. More and more mushroom varieties are being sold in supermarkets, but the two best – porcini (or ceps) and morels-remain rare and expensive. Shiitakes, which can be found everywhere, are excellent substitutes.

Dried porcini, black trumpets and morels are all fairly easy to find and extremely easy to store. When combined with fresh shiitakes or even button mushrooms, the flavour is cranked up a notch. To reconstitute dried mushrooms: soak in very hot water to cover for 10 or 15 minutes, or until soft. Change the water if they are not softening quickly enough, but reserve the soaking water for use in sauces, stocks and stews (strain it first; it's often sandy). Trim the hard parts from the mushrooms and use as you would fresh.

NAM PLA (or nuoc mam; Asian fish sauce): as Jean-Georges calls it, the secret weapon. First, a warning: no one brought up outside of Asia likes the smell of raw nam pla at first. But when you begin to appreciate its power, you'll come to love it. This inexpensive, pungent liquid is made in Thailand, Vietnam, Korea, the Philippines, and elsewhere and used as an all-purpose seasoning. Buy it in Asian supermarkets; it keeps, unrefrigerated, indefinitely.

OIL: Jean-Georges uses two oils regularly: extra virgin olive oil and grapeseed oil. The former is sold everywhere and needs no explanation. The latter is a light, neutral-flavoured oil that is becoming more common but remains expensive and difficult to find; substitute vegetable corn oil, but make sure it is fresh and clean.

PALM SUGAR: the reduced and dried sap of palm trees, this is not unlike the maple sugar sold in New England, which makes a good substitute. More common, much easier and quite acceptable, is brown sugar.

RICE NOODLES: shaped like wheat noodles, but made from rice flour and pale white (sometimes translucent). These require no cooking and can simply be soaked before using, but Jean-Georges likes to soak, then boil them briefly in water to remove all traces of rawness.

RICE PAPER: thin, usually round sheets made from rice flour, which are briefly soaked and used as wrappers, just like flour tortillas. They need no cooking.

SALT: although Jean-Georges usually cooks with regular table salt, he often finishes dishes with a sprinkling of coarse salt. For this, use Maldon sea salt or the exquisite *fleurs de sel*, a special coarse sea salt from France.

SPICES (see also individual spices): best bought whole, which has three advantages: whole spices are less expensive than ground ones. Whole spices retain flavour far better than ground ones. And whole spices can be toasted and ground on the spot (see Spice Grinder, below) for maximum flavour.

TAMARIND: a large brown pod filled with seeds and pulp. Only the pulp is used and its great flavour (yet to be widely appreciated here) is somewhere in between that of prunes and lemons. Usually sold (in some supermarkets and all Asian stores) as a pulp, which contains seeds. This must be made into a seedless purée before using; see page 95 for directions. It's also possible to find tamarind pulp in Asian stores, which can save you a step. Both keep well in the refrigerator.

THE RECIPES IN THIS BOOK ASSUME THE FOLLOWING:

Eggs are large or extra-large.

Butter is salted or unsalted, except in desserts where 'sweet' or unsalted butter should be used.

Flour is plain unless otherwise specified.

Citrus juices-lemon, lime, orange, grapefruit-are freshly squeezed.

Cream, unless specified, is double; milk may be whole or semi-skimmed.

EQUIPMENT

MANDOLINE: An important tool in Jean-Georges's kitchen, the mandoline – a manual slicer that works wonders – was once too expensive for all but the most dedicated (and wealthy) home cooks. But plastic mandolines, made in Japan, cost less than £20/A$50, and are now more common in professional kitchens than the steel French variety. After good knives and cookware, probably the most valuable tool you can buy.

SPICE GRINDER: Jean-Georges makes mixtures from whole spices, which he toasts (for extra flavour) and grinds. You can grind spices in a mortar and pestle or in an electric coffee grinder. But unless you want your coffee to taste like cardamom (not bad) or cumin (yuk), buy a second machine – they cost less than £10/A$25.

TECHNIQUES

TO REMOVE THE PULP FROM A TOMATO: first, skin the tomato by making a small 'x' in the flower (smooth) end and dropping it into boiling water until the skin loosens, about 30 seconds. Drop into iced water, drain and peel. Then use a knife to cut curved longitudinal slices off the core of the tomato.

 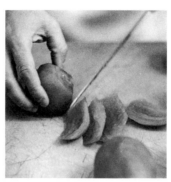

TO CUT UP A LIME FOR JUICING: limes have a solid core which makes cutting them in half for juicing inefficient. The best way to get all the juice out of a lime is to cut it into thirds. First, remove a thin slice from each end; then cut a thick piece about one-third of the way through the lime (1). Turn the lime and cut another slice (2). Finally, cut a third slice, leaving the core intact (3).

TO CUT UP A CHICKEN FOR SAUTEING: Jean-Georges has an efficient way of butchering a chicken, which results in eight pieces, all of which have a good chunk of meat and a bit of bone. Once you learn the technique, it's easy: first, cut off the wing tips and first joint (1) (these are best reserved for stock, although you can cook them in the sauté if you like). Next, cut through some of the breast meat above the wing to remove the wing (2). Find the joint where the thigh meets the carcass (3), and bend it back to pop it out of the socket (4). Remove the leg, beginning with the nugget of meat on the back (5). Stand the carcass up and hack the breast off the back (6); reserve the back for stock. Cut the breast cross-wise into two pieces (7). Hack the knobby bone off of the bottom of each leg (8), and reserve for stock, then cut the leg-thigh pieces in two, right through the joint (9).

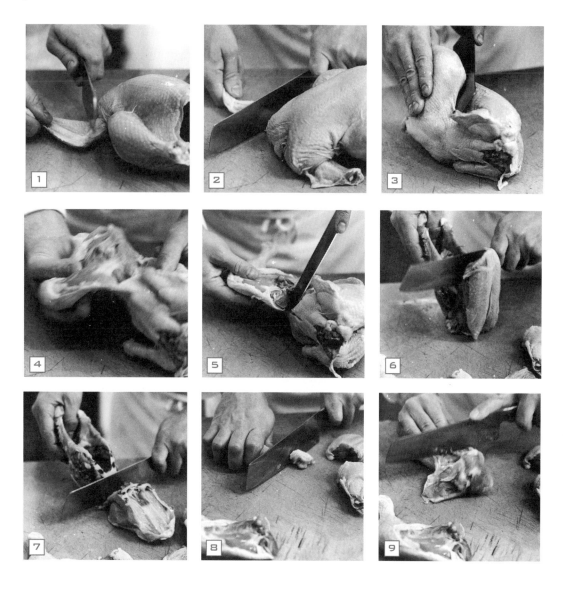

TRIMMING LEMONGRASS: peel the outer sheath from the stalk, as you would the outer layer of a spring onion. Cut the stalk into several lengths (1). Then either whack each with the back of a knife or mince it finely (2).

MINCING GARLIC: Jean-Georges's shortcut for mincing garlic: cut each clove in half, then mash it with the *back* of a knife, using the same motion you would for mincing; this produces a sort of paste. Finish by mincing as usual.

USING A MANDOLINE: there's only one trick to using a mandoline: keep your fingers clear.

A stock in which nothing is chopped or browned. This has the mild but rich flavour of chicken and vegetables, but none of the dark, roasted complexity of Dark Chicken Stock, which follows.

RICH CHICKEN STOCK

1 medium onion, peeled

6 cloves

3 garlic cloves, cut in half

1kg/2lb chicken wings

1 carrot, peeled

1 bay leaf

1 celery stalk

3 or 4 thyme sprigs

1 leek, trimmed and washed

1 Stud the onion with the cloves, then combine all the ingredients in a large saucepan or small stockpot with 2.25l/3¾ pints water. Turn the heat to medium-high and bring to the boil. As soon as bubbles start coming to the surface, adjust the heat so that the mixture cooks at a steady simmer, but not a rapid boil.

2 Cook, covered, for about 1½ hours, stirring occasionally. Cool slightly, then strain, pressing lightly on the solids to extract some of their liquid (don't press too hard or you will cloud the mixture unnecessarily). Use immediately, or refrigerate for up to 3 days, or freeze for up to 3 months.

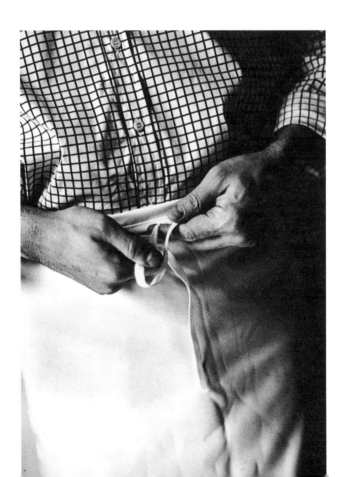

This is close to a classic brown stock, or *jus rôti*. Here you want to brown the meat and cook it quickly, to give you the flavour of roasted meat, not of bones.

You can use this technique with meaty veal or beef bones, or those

MAKES ABOUT 900ML/1 ½ PINTS of rabbit or duck.

DARK CHICKEN STOCK

1 tablespoon vegetable, grapeseed or other neutral-flavoured oil

1kg/2lb chicken wings or other meaty chicken pieces, roughly chopped

1 medium onion, chopped

3 garlic cloves, cut in half

1 carrot, peeled and chopped

1 celery stalk, chopped

1 Preheat the oven to 220°C/450°F/gas 8. Place a roasting tin over high heat on top of the stove and add the oil. A minute later, add the chicken pieces and place the tin in the oven. Stir from time to time, but don't worry about bones sticking to the bottom. The chicken will give up its liquid and then become dark and dry.

2 After about 45 minutes, add the vegetables. Roast for 15 minutes, then stir. Roast for another 15 minutes, then stir again and add 900ml/1½ pints water. Stir and scrape the stuck bits of chicken off the bottom of the pan. Roast for 20 minutes more.

3 Cool, then strain, pressing on the solids to extract as much liquid as possible. Use immediately, or refrigerate for up to 3 days, or freeze for up to 3 months.

Rich Chicken Stock (page 195) or Dark Chicken Stock (page 196) are frequently used when cooking from this book to give the dishes depth of flavour. But when you're making one of the chicken sautés on pages 86–89 and you don't have any stock on hand, you can use the scraps from the cut-up chicken to make this quick chicken stock.

Since you'll often be further reducing the stock while you're cooking it in the specific recipe, it will gain greatly in intensity and give satisfactory results.

MAKES 900ML/1 ½ PINTS

CHICKEN STOCK À LA MINUTE

About 500g/1lb chicken parts

1 carrot, peeled and roughly chopped

1 celery stalk

1 small well-washed leek or peeled onion, or both

Few thyme or parsley sprigs

1 Combine all the ingredients with 900ml/1½ pints water in a large saucepan cover, and bring to the boil.

2 Adjust the heat so that the mixture bubbles, but not furiously, and cook, covered, for 30 minutes. Strain, pressing on the solids to extract all their juices. Use immediately, or refrigerate for up to 3 days, or freeze for up to 3 months.

Having written a cookbook on fish, I know a thing or two about fish stock-or fish fumet as Jean-Georges

calls it – but, as usual, he was able to teach me even more.

Sweating the vegetables for a couple of minutes, adding the

ginger and orange, and using sweet wine all combine to make a

MAKES ABOUT 900ML/1 ½ PINTS broth so delicious (and so nonfishy) you can drink it.

FISH FUMET

1 tablespoon butter or olive oil

1 carrot, peeled and roughly chopped

1 leek, white part only, trimmed, washed, and roughly chopped

1 celery stalk, trimmed and roughly chopped

3 nickel-sized slices of ginger

2 ribbons orange zest

Salt

125ml/4fl oz sweet or dry white wine

500g/1lb bones and/or cleaned heads from any white-fleshed fish

1 bay leaf

1 Place the butter or oil in a deep frying pan or broad saucepan and turn the heat to high. Add the carrot, leek, celery, ginger, orange zest and a big pinch of salt. Cook, stirring, for about 5 minutes, until the vegetables soften.

2 Add the wine and continue to cook over high heat until it is reduced by half, about 2 minutes. Add the fish bones and/or heads, the bay leaf and 900ml/1½ pints water. Cook for 30 minutes at a medium, but not furious, boil.

3 Turn off the heat, then cool the broth for about 15 minutes. Strain and use immediately, or refrigerate for up to 3 days, or freeze for up to 4 weeks.

This aromatic broth is named after a cook who mistakenly added chicken stock instead of water to simmering vegetables.

It's sweeter and more flavourful than any chicken stock, not always appropriate, but just the thing for some dishes, such as Salmon in Cardamom Broth (page 79).

MAKES ABOUT 900ML/1 ½ PINTS

'JACQUELINE' BROTH

25g/1oz butter

1 large onion, roughly chopped

3 celery stalks, roughly chopped

2 medium carrots, roughly chopped

1 leek, white part only, trimmed, washed, and roughly chopped

Salt

900ml/1½ pints dry white wine

900ml/1½ pints Rich Chicken Stock (page 195) or any chicken stock

1 Melt the butter in a deep frying pan or saucepan over medium-high heat. Add the vegetables and a pinch of salt and cook, stirring, until the vegetables are tender, about 10 minutes; adjust the heat as necessary so they do not brown.

2 Add the wine and reduce over medium-high heat until there are 470ml/16fl oz of liquid remaining; this will take 10 to 15 minutes. Add the stock and bring to the boil over high heat, then reduce the heat to medium-high, and cook until it reduces by about one-third; you want just about 900ml/1½ pints of liquid.

3 Put the broth through a fine sieve, pushing down on the vegetables to extract as much juice as possible. Use immediately, or refrigerate for up to 3 days, or freeze for up to 3 months.

A lip-smacking, tart, all-purpose dipping sauce for shrimps or fish, or roasted or grilled chicken or other poultry.

TAMARIND KETCHUP

250g/½lb tamarind pulp (available at Asian markets, or see Note)

2 garlic cloves, very finely minced, almost to a purée

2 or 3 Thai chillies, finely minced

2 tablespoons sugar

2 tablespoons nam pla or nuoc mam (Asian fish sauce)

1 Combine the tamarind pulp with the garlic, chillies, sugar, and nam pla. Set aside for an hour; the flavour will 'grow' during that period. Taste and adjust the seasoning as necessary. This keeps for weeks in the refrigerator.

TAMARIND DIPPING SAUCE

Jean-Georges serves this with Crab Spring Rolls (page 16), and when you try them together you'll see why. Place 250m/9fl oz of Tamarind Ketchup in a blender and add 1 garlic clove, 1 Thai chilli, stemmed, 125ml/4fl oz white vinegar, and 4 tablespoons of nam pla. Blend. With the machine running, slowly add 125ml/4fl oz vegetable or other neutral-flavoured oil. Taste and add more Tamarind Ketchup if you like.

NOTE:

To make tamarind purée, place 500g/1lb tamarind pulp (available at Asian markets) in a saucepan with 250ml/9fl oz water and turn the heat to medium. Cook, whisking lightly to break up the lumps, and adding more water whenever the mixture becomes dry, until you've added a total of about 470ml/16fl oz. The process will take about 10 minutes; the result will be quite thick, but fairly smooth. Put the tamarind through a food mill; you will have about 250ml/9fl oz of purée.

Essential as a dipping sauce for Rice Paper Rolls of Shrimps and Herbs (page 14), this also lends a flavour boost to steamed vegetables, white rice, or grilled meats.

MAKE ABOUT 75ML/3FL OZ

5-MINUTE DIPPING SAUCE

1 tablespoon lime juice

1 tablespoon nam pla or nuoc mam (Asian fish sauce)

1 rounded teaspoon peeled and minced ginger

¼ teaspoon fresh minced chillie, cayenne, or dried red pepper flakes

1 teaspoon sugar

1 Combine all the ingredients in a small bowl. Add 1 tablespoon of water and stir to dissolve the sugar.

2 Taste and adjust the seasonings as necessary. If time allows, let the sauce sit for 15 to 30 minutes before serving to allow the flavours to meld. This sauce will retain its flavour, covered and refrigerated, for about a day; let the sauce come to room temperature before using.

Inspired by a recipe from French chef Joel Robuchon, this is more than a fanciful use of ketchup, but a quick all-purpose sauce that really comes into its own on fish.

MAKES ABOUT 350ML/12FL OZ Serve it hot or warm.

SPICY KETCHUP SAUCE

8 tablespoons ketchup

125ml/4fl oz soy sauce

125ml/4fl oz red wine vinegar

125g/4oz butter

Tabasco

1 Combine all the ingredients in a medium saucepan, adding the Tabasco to taste. Turn the heat to medium and bring to the boil, whisking frequently.

2 Place in a blender and blend until smooth. Serve immediately or refrigerate for up to 3 days; reheat before serving.

This dip has greeted customers at Vong since Day One.

Serve it warm, with thick, square and sweet rice crackers, such as

or raw vegetables.

VONG PEANUT SAUCE

175g/6oz roasted unsalted peanuts

1 tablespoon peanut oil

1 teaspoon curry or vindaloo paste, available at Asian markets; or use All-Purpose Curry Powder (page 214) or commercial curry powder

1 tablespoon sugar

One can (400ml/14fl oz) coconut milk

50ml/2fl oz soy sauce

1 tablespoon lime juice

1 Place the peanuts in a food processor and pulse until crushed; be careful not to purée them.

2 Place the peanut oil in a medium saucepan over medium heat; add the curry paste and whisk for 30 seconds. Whisk in the sugar and coconut milk and cook over medium-low heat, whisking, until smooth and thick, about 5 minutes. Do not boil. Add the crushed peanuts.

3 Add the soy sauce and lime juice; taste and add more sugar, soy or lime if necessary. Keep the sauce warm until you're ready to serve it. If you refrigerate it (it will keep for a couple of days), reheat gently before serving.

Here Jean-Georges takes a sauce from Louis Outhier, his one-time mentor, and adds lemongrass to it, creating an East-West concoction that goes well with Shrimp Satay (page 17). It's great with any fried fish dish.

OYSTER SAUCE

25g/1oz butter

1 large shallot, minced

Salt

1 stalk lemongrass, trimmed and smacked in several places with the back of a knife

1 small fresh chillie, slashed once or twice with a paring knife

250ml/9fl oz dry white wine

6 oysters

250ml/9fl oz cream

Cayenne pepper (optional)

1 Combine the butter and shallot in a small saucepan and turn the heat to medium; add about 1/4 teaspoon salt and cook for about 5 minutes, until the shallot softens.

2 Add the lemongrass (cut it into 2 or 3 pieces if necessary to fit into the pan) and the chilli and cook for another minute. Add the wine and increase the heat to high; cook, stirring only occasionally, until nearly dry, about 5 minutes. You want roughly 2 tablespoons of liquid remaining.

3 Meanwhile, shuck the oysters over a bowl to catch all their liquid. Scrape the oysters, with any of their remaining liquid, into the bowl. Remove the oysters and chop them finely, then return them to the bowl with the liquid.

4 When the wine has reduced sufficiently, add the cream. Bring to the boil, then reduce the heat to low. Taste and add more salt and/or cayenne, if necessary. Stir in the oysters and their liquid and simmer for 10 seconds. Remove the lemongrass and chilli and serve immediately.

This sweet-and-spicy chutney-made with kumquats, that small, oval citrus whose peel is better than its flesh-is good enough to eat with a spoon.

Jean-Georges serves this with many grilled meats and even occasionally as a simple stuffing for split and grilled lobster. Make it a day or two in advance for best flavour.

MAKES ABOUT 900ML/1 ½ PINTS

KUMQUAT-PINEAPPLE CHUTNEY

500g/1lb kumquats

About 750g/1½lb pineapple

1 whole nutmeg

2 teaspoons coriander seeds

2 teaspoons nigella (optional)

1 teaspoon freshly ground black pepper

2 tablespoons palm or brown sugar

1 Place the kumquats in a pan of cold water and bring to the boil. Drain and repeat. Drain and refresh in cold water. Cut in half and remove the insides with your fingers; work over a bowl to save the juice. Combine the juice and the skins; discard the insides. Pulse the skins and juice in a food processor to dice; do not purée.

2 Peel the pineapple and, working around the core, remove all the flesh. Dice into 5mm/¼in cubes.

3 Toast the spices in a dry frying pan over medium heat until they become aromatic, about 3 minutes. Grind them together.

4 Combine the fruit, 1 tablespoon of the spice mixture (reserve the rest), and the sugar in a saucepan. Cook over medium heat until most of the liquid evaporates, for about 20 minutes. Taste and add more spices, if you like. Refrigerate, covered, until ready to use. This keeps well for up to a week; bring to room temperature before serving.

Jean-Georges, combing through a seventeenth-century cookbook, found a recipe combining pineapple,

pears and spices.

He tinkered with it for weeks before settling on this combination,

which complements many grilled foods, from pork to chicken to

MAKES ABOUT 470ML/16FL OZ tuna.

PINEAPPLE-PEAR RELISH

125g/4oz minced pineapple, preferably fresh, but canned is okay

1 ripe but not too soft pear, peeled, cored, and minced

1 Granny Smith apple, peeled, cored, and minced

1½ tablespoons minced ginger

2 tablespoons raisins

½ teaspoon cumin seeds

2½ tablespoons rice vinegar

2 tablespoons brown sugar

2 tablespoons peeled, destemmed, and minced red capsicum pepper

1 Place all the ingredients in a saucepan, mix well, and cover. Bring to the boil over high heat and uncover.

2 Reduce the heat to medium or medium-low and simmer for 15 minutes, stirring occasionally.

3 Remove the relish from the heat and cool to room temperature before serving. This keeps well, covered and refrigerated, for at least a week; bring back to room temperature before serving.

Like the following recipe for Cold Basil Sauce for Fish, this is designed to be served cold over hot fish.

Here, however, you have the sharp, sour taste of sorrel and a dash

of Tabasco.

COLD SORREL SAUCE
FOR FISH

1 egg

About 175g/6oz loosely packed sorrel leaves, roughly chopped

Salt

Tabasco

5 tablespoons vegetable, grapeseed or other neutral-flavoured oil

1 Bring a small pot of water to the boil. Pierce the broad end of the egg with a pin, then gently lower it into the boiling water. Reduce the heat to a simmer and cook for 6 minutes (if large) to 7 minutes (if extra-large). Run the egg under cold water until cool enough to peel, then peel gently (don't worry if the egg breaks) and place in a blender.

2 Add 2½ tablespoons water, the sorrel, salt to taste, and about ¼ teaspoon Tabasco to the blender. Turn the machine on and, while it is running, drizzle in the oil.

3 Leave the sauce to sit for about 10 minutes before tasting and adjusting the seasoning. Refrigerate for up to an hour before using; serve cold.

A quick, simple sauce that marries perfectly with any sautéed or roasted fish.

Especially nice when served along with artichokes cooked as in

MAKES ENOUGH FOR
4 PIECES OF FISH

Sautéed Shrimps with Orange Dust (page 18).

COLD BASIL SAUCE
FOR FISH

2 eggs

90ml/3fl oz extra virgin olive oil

25g/1oz minced basil

Salt and freshly ground black pepper

1 tablespoon lemon juice

1 Bring a small pot of water to the boil. Pierce the broad end of each egg with a pin, then gently lower it into the boiling water. Reduce the heat to a simmer and cook for 6 minutes (if large) to 7 minutes (if extra-large). Run the eggs under cold water until cool enough to peel, then peel gently (don't worry if the eggs break) and place in a bowl.

2 Mash the eggs, then whisk in the olive oil until the mixture is quite thick. Stir in the basil, salt and pepper to taste and lemon juice and serve.

If you have Cherry Vinegar (page 209) – which is worth waiting for – by all means use it. But if you didn't plan

two weeks ahead and want this vinaigrette now, use red wine vinegar; the results will be fine.

Dress any salad with this brightly coloured vinaigrette, or drizzle it

MAKES ABOUT 250ML/9FL OZ   on grilled fish or shrimps or raw oysters.

CHERRY VINAIGRETTE

5 cardamom pods

5cm/2in piece of cinnamon stick

10 black peppercorns, lightly crushed

250ml/9fl oz port

150g/5oz cherries, preferably sour but sweet will do fine

125ml/4fl oz cherry vinegar (page 209) or red wine vinegar

Salt and freshly ground black pepper

6 tablespoons vegetable, grapeseed or other neutral-flavoured oil

1 Break the cardamom pods and put them, hulls and all, in a medium saucepan with the cinnamon, peppercorns and port. Bring to the boil over high heat and add the cherries. Cook over medium-high heat, stirring occasionally. After 5 minutes or so, crush the cherries with the back of a spoon.

2 Continue to cook until the mixture has formed a thick syrup, a total of about 15 minutes. Strain, pressing on the solids to extract as much liquid as possible. You should have about 4 tablespoons of liquid. (If you have significantly more, return the liquid to the saucepan and reduce a little further, stirring frequently.)

3 Place the mixture in a bowl, then whisk in the vinegar, salt and lots of freshly ground black pepper and the oil. Serve immediately or store, covered and refrigerated, for a day or two; bring back to room temperature before serving.

Not only is this intense vinegar preferred for Cherry Vinaigrette (page 208), you get the cherries as a bonus.

As Jean-Georges says, 'They're terrific with a pastrami sandwich

MAKES ABOUT 250ML/9FL OZ,
PLUS SOME CHERRIES instead of a pickle.'

CHERRY VINEGAR

250ml/9fl oz white vinegar

300g/10oz cherries, washed, stems removed

1 Bring the vinegar to the boil. Put the cherries in a heatproof container and pour the still-hot vinegar over them.

2 Cool, then refrigerate for at least 2 weeks, with the cherries still in the vinegar. This will keep, refrigerated, indefinitely.

This is Jean-Georges's basic vinaigrette, an all-purpose dressing in which the honey not only tames the garlic but adds wonderful body and, of course, sweetness.

MAKES ABOUT 150ML/5FL OZ Fine for salads or drizzling over grilled meat or chicken.

HONEY-GARLIC VINAIGRETTE

4 tablespoons balsamic vinegar

1 tablespoon honey

½ teaspoon very finely minced garlic

8 tablespoons extra virgin olive oil

Salt and freshly ground black pepper

1 Use a small wire whisk to combine the vinegar and honey in a small bowl; add the garlic and stir.

2 Still whisking, add the oil a little at a time. Season to taste and use immediately or refrigerate for up to 2 days; whisk or shake up before using.

The unusual combination of ginger and olive oil may surprise you, but it certainly works. For best flavour,

make this a day in advance.

MAKES ENOUGH FOR AT LEAST
SALAD FOR 6

Wonderful on greens or drizzled on fish.

GINGER VINAIGRETTE

250ml/9fl oz extra virgin olive oil

5cm/2in piece of ginger, peeled and roughly chopped

1 tablespoon sherry vinegar

2 tablespoons lime juice

Salt and freshly ground black pepper

1 Combine all the ingredients in a blender, using plenty of black pepper. Add 1 tablespoon of warm water. Blend until the sauce is emulsified.

2 Leave to rest for a day before using, if possible. This will keep, covered and refrigerated, for several days; let the dressing come to room temperature before using.

Another all-purpose vinaigrette, this one light and fresh-tasting. The secret ingredient: a tablespoon of hot

water, which helps the mixture emulsify and makes it creamy.

MAKES ABOUT 250ML/9FL
OZ

LEMON VINAIGRETTE

Juice of 2 or 3 lemons

Salt and freshly ground black pepper

8 tablespoons extra virgin olive oil

1 Place the lemon juice, salt and plenty of pepper in a blender. Turn on the machine and gradually add the oil.

2 When all the oil has been incorporated, add 1 tablespoon of hot water and blend until the mixture is creamy. Adjust the seasoning and use. Or refrigerate the dressing for up to a day; bring to room temperature and blend again before using.

The backbone of Sautéed Shrimps with Orange Dust (page 18), this homemade dust was devised by Didier Virot, formerly chef at JoJo and now chef de cuisine at Jean-Georges.

You can use the same technique to make lemon or lime dust, and use any of these as seasoning for sautéed, grilled, or roasted meat, fish, or poultry. Orange dust sometimes can be purchased in shops, but the flavour doesn't come close to the homemade version.

MAKES 2 OR 3
TABLESPOONS OF DUST

 # ORANGE DUST

2 oranges

4 tablespoons sugar

½ teaspoon vegetable, grapeseed or other neutral-flavoured oil

1 Use a vegetable peeler to peel the oranges; you should get 8 or 10 broad strips from each one. Scrape all the white pith from inside the peel using a paring knife. Preheat the oven to 180°C/350°F/gas 4.

2 Place the peels in a small saucepan with 250ml/9fl oz of water and the sugar. Turn the heat to high, then reduce to medium when the liquid begins to boil. When it becomes syrupy, 10 to 15 minutes later, remove the peels and drain them.

3 Line a baking sheet with aluminum foil and spread the oil on the foil. Scatter the cooked peels on the sheet; they should not touch one another.

4 Bake until dry, but not at all brown, for about 15 minutes (if they begin to brown before they are dry, reduce the oven heat). Leave to cool at room temperature, preferably in a dry place.

5 Crumble, then grind in a spice mill or coffee grinder until powdery. Store in a tightly sealed jar. Orange dust retains peak flavour for a couple of weeks, but it will keep virtually forever, gradually losing intensity.

Compound butter taken to the next level: it starts out as if you are making a béarnaise sauce, but the flavoured vinegar is used to set off mustard.

It's a lovely combination; use it on roast beef sandwiches or with

Cumin Crisps (page 54).

MUSTARD BUTTER

2 tablespoons minced shallot

8 tablespoons red wine vinegar

1 tablespoon minced fresh tarragon or 1 teaspoon dried

50g/2oz butter, softened

2 tablespoons grainy mustard, such as Moutarde de Meaux

Salt and freshly ground black pepper

1 Combine the shallot, vinegar and tarragon in a small saucepan and turn the heat to medium-high. Boil, stirring occasionally, until the shallot is just moist.

2 Meanwhile, cream the butter with the mustard. When the reduction is ready, cool it off, then add it to the butter. Season to taste with salt and pepper and serve at once, or refrigerate in an airtight container for up to a week.

Just as we were finishing this book, Jean-Georges began to serve sourdough white and rye breads at Restaurant Jean-Georges. The huge loaves weigh nearly 4kg/8lb each, and the restaurant goes through about thirty each day, slicing them by hand. Because the breads are so well-done and crisp, there were lots of dark brown, crackling bread crumbs left at the end of the day. Unable to throw them away, Jean-Georges made it his business to work out a use for these strongly flavoured crumbs. The result is a puréed sauce of mahogany colour and stunningly complex flavour. Those who taste it, unaware of the ingredients, think it contains a meat stock and mushrooms or even foie gras.

It's at its best on roasted birds, but it is also good on sturdy fish, such as monkfish or red snapper. Chances are good you won't have as many leftover breadcrumbs as Jean-Georges does, but the sauce can also be made with good-quality French bread.

MAKES ENOUGH FOR 4

BURNT BREAD SAUCE

2 slices good French bread

2 tablespoons butter

2 large shallots, minced

50g/2oz prosciutto or other dry-cured ham, with some of its fat, cut into large chunks

Salt and freshly ground black pepper

50g/2oz pecans

1 tablespoon sherry or balsamic vinegar

1 Preheat the oven to 250°C/475°F/gas 9. Chop the bread into small pieces, not more than 1.2cm/½in in any dimension. Bake for 10 to 12 minutes, until the pieces are dark brown, almost burned. Remove from the oven.

2 Place 1 tablespoon of butter in a medium saucepan, turn the heat to medium-high, and add the shallots, along with the prosciutto and a sprinkling of salt. Cook, stirring, until the shallots soften, for about 5 minutes. Add the bread and 470ml/16fl oz of water and simmer for 20 minutes.

3 Add the pecans to the sauce and bring back to the boil. Cool slightly, then remove and discard the ham. Purée the sauce in a blender until perfectly smooth. Reheat and stir in the remaining 1 tablespoon of butter and the vinegar. Add salt and pepper to taste. (This sauce can be made a day in advance and stored in the refrigerator; it will improve in flavour as it sits.) Serve the sauce hot.

This is a fairly mild curry powder and an enchantingly fragrant one. It is superb in Curried Mussels (page 59), and any other dish requiring curry powder.

Like all of the other spice mixtures in this book, it will keep for

MAKES ABOUT 4 TABLESPOONS months in an opaque covered container.

ALL-PURPOSE CURRY POWDER

1 star anise

6 cardamom pods

3 cloves

¹/₂ teaspoon cumin seeds

2 teaspoons coriander seeds

¹/₄ teaspoon cayenne

¹/₂ teaspoon mace pieces or ground mace

¹/₂ teaspoon whole or ground fenugreek

1 teaspoon white peppercorns

2 teaspoons ground turmeric

1 Place all the whole spices in a small saucepan or frying pan and toast over medium heat, shaking the pan frequently, until fragrant, about 3 minutes. Cool.

2 Combine the toasted and powdered spices in a spice grinder and whirr to a powder. Store in a covered opaque container.

This seasoning paste serves as the basis for the Sweet-and-Sour Sauce, which is the best dip for the Shrimp Satay (page 17). Vietnamese chilli-garlic paste, sold in most Asian markets, is a decent substitute, although it does contain preservatives.

If you can't find 'finger' chillies – which are not super – hot-mix small jalapeños or Thai chillies with sweet capsicum peppers to achieve a moderate but assertive level of heat.

MAKES ABOUT 250ML/9FL OZ

VONG CHILLI PASTE

250g/½lb long, hot 'finger' chillies

1 tablespoon sugar

Scant 90ml/3fl oz white vinegar

2 garlic cloves

1 tablespoon nam pla or nuoc mam (Asian fish sauce)

1 Destem the chillies, then chop them roughly. Place them in a blender or food processor with the sugar, vinegar, garlic and nam pla. Blend until the ingredients are minced, but not puréed.

2 Taste and adjust the seasoning if necessary; the mixture should be quite hot, with all other flavours present but definitely in the background.

SWEET-AND-SOUR SAUCE

To 250ml/9fl oz of Vong Chilli Paste, stir in 5–6 tablespoons of honey, an additional tablespoon of nam pla, and the juice of 1 lime.

INDEX